WEIRDER WAR TWO

WEIRDER WAR TWO

RICHARD DENHAM

&

MICHAEL JECKS

'In wartime, truth is so precious that she should always be attended by a bodyguard of lies.'

- Winston Churchill

FOREWORD

Both world wars have influenced me since my earliest years, I think it's fair to say.

In part, that's probably partly because I was born only 15 years after the end of the Second World War - and much of the countryside around me in the South East was still pocked with craters caused by the bombs dropped by German aircraft who couldn't find their targets and dare not land with their payload still aboard.

I can remember visiting London and seeing the remains of many buildings. Even in 1980 there was still a massive gap in the buildings just north of Ludgate. That one wasn't filled until the mid-80s, when a new British Telecom building was installed on the site. So through my early years and teens the damage caused by the war was visible on all sides.

No doubt the number of uncles and friends who had served also affected me. Although very few would discuss their experiences, it was something for a small boy to wonder about, when he heard that this man had served in this regiment, and had seen action from

D-Day, or on the march through Burma (Burma? Where's Burma?). It was a matter of great pride to me that, after publishing my first six novels, my father's great friend, Don Morton, asked me to type up his memoirs.

However, most of my interest probably came from the fact that I was born on November 11th. That accident of fate was enough to inspire me to study the wars and try to understand them.

From nine or ten years old, I was reading about the history of war. I well remember going to school on the train while reading *The First Day on the Somme* by Martin Middlebrook (Allen Lane, 1971) when I was ten years old, and moving from that to Basil Liddell Hart's *History of the First World War* and Churchill's *The Second World War*. I was fully immersed in my subject before finding a photographic encyclopedia of the Second World War in the school library.

That was an astonishing find, for me. I would regularly slip away during lunchtimes to delve into the book. There was much in there that has remained with me - in particular the repellent pictures of mounds of corpses found at the concentration camps. My loathing of Holocaust deniers and anti-Semitism was founded in that library.

When I was still only twelve years old, the main British commercial television channel started to broadcast a new series: *The World At War*. This was groundbreaking television. Narrated by Sir Laurence Olivier, it relied on first-hand interviews with participants from all the main armies. There were members of the German headquarters staff, men who had helped plan the Japanese assaults, soldiers and civilians who had lived through the Blitz, others who escaped the slaughter at Nanjing, men and women from the siege of Stalingrad and survivors of the concentration camps, all intermixed with rare footage from the time. For me, it was astonishing and deeply moving: a story told with enormous skill and sympathy.

But of course it was not detailed. How could it be? Both the nature of television, with one hour slots (which had to include advert breaks), and the secrecy that still prevailed only twenty five or thirty years after the War, meant that it could not be exhaustive. Then again, when some interviews were conducted it is clear in retrospect that those discussing certain situations were justifying their own actions.

There is a perfect example of the impact of secrecy on the programme: when it mentioned the war against the U-Boats, there was no mention of Bletchley Park and the codebreakers who did so much to help track down the submariners and destroy them. Everything about Bletchley Park was still hidden because of the Official Secrets Act. It was notable that the men and women who worked there kept their secrets. Many took them to their graves, while others would only talk when the public became aware of their efforts in, I think, the 1990s.

But in the midst of the self-justifications, the understandable attempts to protect secrets, the stories of disasters and "friendly fire", there are many tales that are less well known and understood.

And so we come to this book.

Is there really anything new that we can discover about the Second World War now? Richard Denham has already written his excellent *Weird War Two* with M.J. Trow, so is there more to expound upon?

Well, sadly, yes. And not only because they are simply interesting, but because there are men and women in these pages who *deserve* to be remembered. Everyone should read of the exploits of Abba Kovner and the FPO, or about the heroism of Desmond Doss and the mad courage of John R. McKinney. But there are also the stories of Judy the Pointer of Shanghai, or Bamse of Norway, and the horrible massacre of British pets in the early days. Animals suffered as well as humans.

There were the fabulous and ridiculous weapons, from Die Glocke, the Fire Hedgehog and death rays, to the Silbervogel. Then there are the stories of a Japanese pilot's attempt to take over a Hawaiian island, the farcical assault by the US to recover the Aleutian Islands, and even the post-war declaration of sovereignty by the independent state of Sealand. There is enough in these pages to inspire laughter, tears and wonder at the sheer inventiveness of man at time of war, but also a cold chill at the horrors.

Richard Denham has an uncanny knack of getting into the nooks and crannies of the conflict. He has researched the war in great detail, and is to be congratulated on this, his latest collection of the fabulous, the heartwarming and the often almost unbelievable.

My thanks go to him for asking me to become involved - and I hope you too enjoy the tales of the curious events of 1939-45.

Michael Jecks

INTRODUCTION

Weird; *out of the ordinary, strange, unusual…odd, bizarre, incomprehensible.*

New Shorter English Dictionary

The prequel to this book, *Weird War Two*, was fascinating to write. The sheer scale of weird and wonderful stories from the period continues to amaze me. Irrefutable facts, apocryphal tales, dubious truths and outright lies still interest us over seventy years later. Even more surprising was the sheer amount of stories that continued to come after the first book was published – enough to fill a second book!

There is no doubt World War Two was a dark place, and there is a peculiarly depressing and draining quality in writing about and researching it. As an example, Philip K. Dick, popular science-fiction writer and author of *Man in the High Castle* tried several times to write a sequel, in the end scrapping it completely. He gave up because he found his research too disturbing and couldn't stomach knowing anything else about the Nazis. Trying to get into the mindset of monsters like Reinhard Heydrich again was just too much.

Philip K. Dick was right. The sheer scale of the horror of it all can be overwhelming, but this also makes the countless stories of humanity, friendship, compassion and courage – many of which will never come to light - even more powerful.

For the dwindling few who are still with us - and many great souls have passed in the short gap between this book and the first - a unique gallows humour developed. Through the horrors of war and the appalling loss of life, people would, somehow, still find reasons to laugh and smile, even if it was just at the absurdity of it all. It was a natural reaction, which to a modern mind could appear cold and callous - but it was healthy, it worked, and it helped get them through it.

It's important to add this book shouldn't be categorised as 'humour'. Many of the tales are dark and distressing. Some of the more sinister stories made me uncomfortable adding them. But apart from a handful, I chose to keep the rest in. These things, though grim, did happen – or at the very least the accounts did happen – and I feel it is important not to censor any history just because it could offend our modern sensibilities.

My hope is that you, the reader, will use this book as a sort of springboard to do your own research on the articles that interest you, make up your own mind and (hopefully) agree just how futile trying to uncover the truth of so many incidents truly is.

With that being said, like the first book, I have tried to keep this one as light-hearted and accessible as possible. Humorous and light moments, when appropriate, are contrasted with horror and tragedy. But the alternative, to not allow humour its role, would be too cold and depressing for writer and reader alike. I can only apologise in advance if anything written causes offence.

Once again, undeniable facts sit alongside rumours and stories that are most certainly false or embellished. This I can't apologise for - tall tales, bravado, misinformation, propaganda and outright lies swirled together during the war and I believe those stories that are doubtful or most certainly false deserve their place. Accounts that *aren't* true can be as telling as those that are, and they help us understand the bigger picture of the conflict. It also helps us to understand why people said what they said, and why certain rumours and hoaxes have followed us through the years. There must be a line where it is assumed that accounts aren't certain. People lie, memories fail, newspapers embellish, governments omit; but it would be unacceptable to fill the pages of each account in this book with the continuous use of words such as possibly, probably, allegedly, maybe and so on.

Even to this day, experts continue to dissect the war and scrap over this period of history, from the tiniest minutiae to major aspects. None of us can help having an agenda, even at a subconscious level. It is human nature. We naturally favour that which we like and overlook inconvenient truths which we don't. It would be a wise one indeed who could hold all the countless tales of the war - Allies, Axis, Soviets and neutrals - together with complete balance and impartiality and without the slightest intention or prejudice.

So what's the truth of any of it? Which sources can we trust, and which can we not? That's what the world has been struggling with for the last seven decades and will continue to do so for a very long time to come.

Below each title, you will find one to three exclamations to demonstrate how weird we personally believe something was, from weird, to weirder, to weirdest.

A huge thank you to the talented Michael Jecks for collaborating with me on this project. His insights, level head and wisdom have been extremely valuable, and I would encourage you to read his other titles.

Welcome, once more, to Weird War Two…

Richard Denham

CONTENTS

THE AVENGERS

!

Abba Kovner was born in Belarus in 1918. By the time of the Second World War, Abba was in Vilna, Lithuania when the Reich conquered it. Abba and his friends, being Jewish and at risk of persecution, went into hiding in a Dominican convent. He was disgusted and outraged with what was happening to people in the Jewish ghetto with thousands of victims having been murdered. Abba had seen first-hand what the Nazis were capable of. But many in the ghettos could not believe the wickedness of it all. Even as the ghettos began to be cleared out, there was much disbelief about the destination and the so-called resettlement.

Abba gave a passionate speech in the ghetto to the surviving remnant:

> 'Jewish youth! Do not trust those who are trying to deceive you. Out of the eighty thousand Jews in the "Jerusalem of Lithuania" only twenty thousand are left. Ponary is not a concentration camp. They

have all been shot there. Hitler plans to destroy all the Jews of Europe, and the Jews of Lithuania have been chosen as the first in line. We will not be led like sheep to the slaughter! True, we are weak and defenceless, but the only reply to the murderer is revolt! Brothers! Better to fall as free fighters than to live by the mercy of the murderers. Arise! Arise with your last breath!'

A group named FPO (United Partisan Organisation) began in January 1942, but many Jewish people feared their resistance was simply antagonising the Nazis and would not openly support it. The FPO soon came to the attention of the Gestapo. It was announced that if their leader, Yitzhak Wittenberg, did not hand himself in, they would kill the 20,000 remaining Jews in the city. Wittenberg did the honourable thing and did in fact hand himself in to save the lives of those he had sworn to protect. Before submitting to certain death he appointed Kovner as the FPO's new leader. Wittenberg would be found dead in his cell the next day on July 16, 1943. Kovner continued the struggle, carrying out acts of sabotage, forging links with the Red Army and sending word to other ghettos not to volunteer themselves onto the trains, as they too would be going to their deaths. By September 1943 the ghettos of Vilna were desolate.

The FPO escaped Vilna and met up with Soviet partisans and continued the fight. As the war was nearing its end, the FPO assisted in helping Jews flee to Palestine via the *Beriha* (Escape) movement. Over 250,000 people would make it.

When the war was finally over, the full scale of the

atrocities committed by the Nazis became evident, and many wanted revenge. The FPO joined forces with sympathetic soldiers from within the Jewish Brigade, a unit made up of war veterans serving in the British Army, and formed *Nakam* (Revenge).

Although many high-ranking Nazis were convicted at the Nuremburg War Trials, countless others escaped punishment in the chaos and confusion of post-war Europe. To those who had suffered, this 'justice' was woefully inadequate. Of an original list of 13 million suspects, by 1949 only 300 would face prison or worse. The prosecution was exhausted and the task in front of them was never ending. The world wanted to forgive and move on – Nakam couldn't. Every member of Nakam had his own story, returning to their homes to find it being lived in by strangers and awkward glances from neighbours who only years before had informed on them to the enemy. This new atmosphere of forgiveness and reconciliation did not sit well with them.

Nakam planned to poison the water supplies of German cities, in the hope of killing six million people. The plan never came to fruition. It is believed this operation, which was appalling in its scale of brutality and arbitrary punishment, was sabotaged or stopped by those overseeing the Nakam operation itself. They feared the world could not support an organisation capable of such a murderous act. Not to mention the hindrance this may pose in the creation of a Jewish nation.

Plan B was the planned poisoning of 15,000 Axis POWs who were being held in an American camp near Nuremburg. A Nakam cell discovered all of the food was prepared on site except for the bread, which came from a nearby bakery where two Nakam agents were able to find work. They pasted 3,000 loaves of bread with arsenic. When it was delivered to the POW camp, the agents fled. After the event, the *New York Times* reported over 2,000 POWs became ill and 400 died as a result, though later evidence suggests the poisoned bread didn't actually kill anyone. Experts claim the poison could have killed 60,000, so it is a mystery as to why this failed.

Nakam gradually faded away as its members found peace and gave up their desire for revenge. Abba Kovner moved to Israel, becoming a renowned poet and eventually retired on a kibbutz where he lived with his wife until his death in 1987.

The morality and justification for the actions and motives of Abba Kovner and Nakam remain a subject of discourse. Some suggest Nakam was a terrorist organisation, though German prosecutors dismissed a case against them due to the 'unusual circumstances' they found themselves in.

Elsewhere, SS officers and high-ranking Nazi officials who had successfully faded back into normal life, were being found dead in suspicious circumstances across the world.

BAMSE THE DOG

!!

Bamse (teddy bear) was a St. Bernard from Norway who refused to let the Nazi occupation of his homeland dampen his spirits. With the coming of war, Bamse and his owner Erling Hafto saw their whale-catcher vessel *Thorodd* drafted into the Norwegian navy. Bamse was officially enrolled on 9th February 1940.

The Nazi war machine devastated Norway and by 10th June the Scandinavian nation was conquered. The British and French mismanagement in failing to aid their ally would lead to the replacement of then Prime Minister, Neville Chamberlain, with the untested Winston Churchill on 10th May. Winston Churchill was a controversial figure and distrusted by many politicians, he had left the Conservative party to join the Liberals in 1904, only to rejoin the Conservatives in 1924. Even worse, he was half-American to boot!

Only thirteen Norwegian naval vessels were able to escape to Britain, *Thorodd* was among them. With French forces crumbling and their government weeks from surrender, the 'lifeboat of democracy' was the last free country in open opposition to Hitler. The vessel was converted into a minesweeper and spent the remainder of the war stationed in Montrose and Dundee in Scotland.

Bamse lead from the front, earning fame and prestige among his crew and the locals thanks to his heroism. In battle, he stood defiantly at the front of the *Thorodd*, wearing his custom-made helmet. He saved the life of Olav August Johan Nilsen, who was walking the docks, by pushing a knife-wielding attacker into the sea. He saved another who had fallen overboard by jumping into the sea and dragging him to shore. He would calm down his crew when tensions got high and scuffles developed by placing a paw on their shoulders. He even rounded up his crew who were due to return from shore leave by travelling on local buses, unaccompanied, with a bus pass attached to his collar. He then turned up at the favourite pub of his men, the Bodega Bar, and escorted his worse-for-wear friends back to their ship. If he didn't find them, that was fine. He'd come back another time.

Bamse passed away in July 1944 and was buried with full military honours in Montrose. He became a mascot for both the Free Norwegian Forces and the charity PDSA (People's Dispensary for Sick Animals). In 2006 a bronze statue of the heroic dog was unveiled on Montrose's Wharf Street, facing Norway. In 2009, the Norwegians erected their own statue of Bamse in Honningsvag, facing Scotland. In 2016, a 17-acre forest, 'Bamse's Wood', in Cumbria was planted in his honour.

THE BATTLE OF SCHOENFELD

!

The Battle of Schoenfeld was the last successful horseback cavalry charge of the Second World War, or since, happening on 1st March 1945.

Attached to Soviet forces, the Polish First Army was assisting in the push to the Baltic Sea. The Germans were dug in at the village of Schoenfeld and it fell to the Polish forces to take it. Infantry forces and tanks were initially unsuccessful in their attack, due to the Germans having anti-tank guns and the advantage of elevation. It was now the turn of the 1st Warsaw Independent Cavalry Brigade. They led a new assault, using a ravine and the smoke of burning tanks to hide their approach.

The charge took the defending Germans completely by surprise, cutting swathes through their ranks. The horsemen then overran anti-tank positions and lead the assault on the village itself. Joined by their infantry and tanks, they forced the defenders to flee.

The Polish lost 147 men, including just seven cavalry, to the Germans loss of 500. A plaque in the village, now called Żeńsko, commemorates the attack.

The fact cavalry were still being used may seem odd enough, but there was also poetic justice in their success. Six years earlier, the Nazis and Soviets had openly mocked the Polish and their supposed reliance on horses. They invented an incident, for the mockery of the world press, that the Polish cavalry had foolishly and suicidally charged panzers.

The age of cavalry was over, but the battle of Schoenfeld was an apt last hurrah.

THE BERLIN OLYMPICS

!

The Olympic Games have a long tradition, going back to ancient Greece. The games were eventually banned by the Romans when they turned to Christianity as they believed them to be a pagan celebration. In these ancient games, fires were lit in the temples of various gods to honour them.

It would be over 1,400 years until the games were reborn as the modern Olympics in 1896. The Olympic flame made its return in the 1928 summer games in Amsterdam. But it was the Nazis, in the 1936 Berlin Olympics, who conceived of the idea of running the torch from Greece to the host nation. Using over 3,000 people, the runners managed the relay in twelve days, where the final runner lit the torch to mark the start of the games. This tradition survives to this day.

As well as giving the world the Olympic Torch, the Berlin Olympics are known for a much better reason. Although much has been made of the black athlete Jesse Owens' historic victories at the 1936 Berlin

Olympics, this is another case that doesn't quite tell the full story. The myth is that Owens winning so many gold medals infuriated Hitler and belittled his claims of Aryan physical supremacy. Adolf was so incensed, he stormed out and a moral victory was gained for black people, democracy and America.

Jesse Owens was in fact warmly received by the German public who cheered his name and congratulated his four gold medals, with admiring fans asking for his autograph. Jesse said the reaction at Berlin was the best he ever received. Hitler *did* refuse to speak to a black athlete, Cornelius Johnson on the first day. But this wasn't personal. Hitler was in attendance and congratulated the German athletes, but the Olympic officials protested the neutrality of the event and insisted he had to receive all the athletes, or none of them. So he chose the latter – and did not congratulate any of the athletes again.

Jesse's victories were on the second day, when Hitler wasn't seeing anyone. Jesse himself was frustrated by the manipulation of the truth and later commented:

'When I passed the Chancellor he arose, waved his hand at me, and I waved back at him. I think the writers showed bad taste in criticizing the man of the hour in Germany.'

The Olympics went better than Hitler could have dreamed, and he was delighted with the results. Not only did Germany win more medals than any other country, Hitler also revelled in such a successful publicity and propaganda campaign.

Some people tried to get the US to boycott the Olympic games, including the American ambassador to Germany, who was well aware of the horrors being committed by the Nazis and the fact it would be an overwhelming victory for Hitler in the propaganda stakes. The opponents to US participation lost the argument.

In fact, it was returning to America where racism was rife, that Jesse Owens faced discrimination. He did receive a ticker tape parade but was soon forgotten by the American people. Three years after Berlin he was declared bankrupt. President Roosevelt received the white athletes from the games but did not invite Jesse to the White House, congratulate him, or acknowledge his victories. According to Jesse's daughter Gloria, when the hero was attending a hotel for his own celebration, he had to use the back door to enter due to the colour of his skin.

What is weird here is that the oppression and persecution stopped in Berlin while the city was hosting the Olympics. It was as if a great, collective, dirty secret was put on hold until the foreigners had left again.

BERNHARD LICHTENBERG

!

Bernhard Lichtenberg was a German Catholic priest who was brave enough to speak out against the Nazis. A veteran of the First World War, Bernard was 62 years old when the persecution of the Jews was being increased, particularly after *Kristallnacht* on 9-10th November 1938. He was also deeply troubled by the euthanasia program, Aktion T4, aimed at disabled and mentally ill people. The priest found the actions of his countrymen repulsive and would courageously end each mass with a prayer for the Jews and other victims of the concentration camps.

He wrote a letter to Leonardo Conti, the chief physician of the Reich in 1942 saying:

'I, as a human being, a Christian, a priest, and a German, demand of you, Chief Physician of the Reich, that you answer for the crimes that have been perpetrated at your bidding, and with your consent, and which will call forth the vengeance of the Lord on the heads of the German people.'

Typically, such dissent could not be tolerated by the Nazis. Lichtenberg was put before the Berlin District Court and found guilty of 'abuse of the pulpit' and other insidious activity. He was sentenced to two years imprisonment.

During this term, Bishop Prysing visited him in prison. He then brokered a deal with the Gestapo allowing Lichtenberg to go free if he refrained from any further anti-Nazi activity. The priest refused, asking instead to be able to serve as a minister in Lodz, Poland.

This was intolerable to the Reich, who ordered his internment in Dachau concentration camp. He never worked a day, though, having died on 5th November 1943, during the train journey there. For his unyielding courage in the face of adversity he was beatified in 1996 by Pope John Paul II and declared as 'righteous among the nations' by Israel.

Leonardo Conti was arrested after the war and would have been put on trial for his involvement in Aktion T4, but he hanged himself in his cell on 6th October 1945, before this trial began.

THE BLACKOUT RIPPER

!

The Blitz has a deservingly prestigious place in British folklore. Through the bombings and terror, the British public generally pulled together with courage, a sense of humour and community which hasn't been seen since, and which is remembered as 'the Blitz spirit'.

In such times, an element of trust was naturally assumed in a person's neighbours. Homes were vulnerable, shops were defenceless and the streets were abandoned. Those who robbed and looted during the blackouts were treated with particular scorn.

One particularly vicious Briton, Gordon Cummins, an RAF serviceman, would use the blackouts and the chaos of bombing as a cover for a brutal murder spree in 1942. His first victim, Evelyn Hamilton, was found gagged and strangled in a West End air raid shelter. The next day saw Evelyn Oatley strangled and slashed across her abdomen with a tin opener in her apartment. The 13th of February saw two more victims, Margaret Lowe and Doris

Jouannet, both alleged prostitutes who suffered equally gruesome deaths.

The newspapers dubbed the killer 'The Blackout Ripper', for his inclination to attack during the blackouts, while most of the city was taking shelter. This, however, made those who did not take shelter such as prostitutes, or 'ladies of the night' particularly vulnerable.

The 14th of February saw two more attacks on Greta Hayward and Kathleen Mulcahy, though both of these victims were able to fight off their attacker and survive the ordeal.

However, the Blackout Ripper would not disappear uncaught into urban legend like his namesake Jack the Ripper, who had terrorized Victorian London fifty years earlier. It was only a matter of time before Cummins slipped up. During his attack on Hayward, he dropped his gas mask case, complete with his serviceman's serial number 525987. Investigators entered his lodgings on the 16th February and arrested Cummins who protested his innocence, though his proclivity for taking a memento from each of his victims was to be his undoing.

Cummins was tried for murder and received the death penalty. In a final dark twist, the Blackout Ripper was hanged by Albert Pierrepoint, ironically during a German air raid.

BRIDE SCHOOLS

!!!

eichsbräuteschule, 'Reich Bride Schools,' were set up by Nazi Germany to train women to become the perfect wives and mothers. It is always hard not to scoff at nonsense like this, and we should try to allow ourselves a pinch of humour when it is appropriate. If you will forgive the mocking tangent, we can almost imagine the lessons of this 'school' as an old fashioned cooking show.

> 'First off ladies, let's make sure there is none of that yucky Jewish or gypsy blood in you. Good, how about any of that horrid physical or mental illness which costs the state so much? You are going to breed healthy children aren't you? Excellent, now if you could just prove your Aryan ancestry back to 1800. Lovely, you truly are on your way to becoming a queen of the hearth and beginning your special task. Now, just grab yourself a tall and handsome SS fiancé and you're ready to begin.'

This 'special task' was to stop working, forget their previous lives and work on their 'spiritual and physical wellbeing'. But before they got to spiritual wellbeing, best to learn how to iron shirts and uniforms properly first. And there was cooking and gardening to be done, and let's not forget to give your husband's boots a once over. Also, make sure to vigorously polish his dagger when he gets home.

Working women were shunned as cold-hearted *Rabenmutter* (Raven mothers), cruelly abandoning their children, pushing them away from the bosom and the hearth.

The Nazi 'ten commandments' of 1934 for choosing a spouse were as follows:

1. Remember that you are a German.
2. If you are hereditarily healthy, you should not remain unmarried.
3. Keep your body pure!
4. You should keep your mind and spirit pure!
5. As a German choose only a spouse of same or Nordic blood.
6. In choosing your spouse, ask about his ancestors.
7. Health is a requirement also for physical beauty.
8. Marry only for love.
9. Seek a companion in marriage and not a playmate.
10. You should wish for as many children as possible.

And for female readers whose blood hasn't quite reached boiling point, six other points were added, particularly for women;

1. Women should not work for a living
2. Women should not wear trousers
3. Women should not wear makeup
4. Women should not wear high-heeled shoes
5. Women should not dye or perm their hair
6. Women should not go on slimming diets

Who said romance is dead?

THE BRITISH PET
MASSACRE

!

In 1939 war was declared, just twenty-one years after the horrors of the Great War that irretrievably changed the world forever. With new threats and technologies available in the new conflict, Britain was taking no chances.

NARPAC, the National Air Raid Precautions Animal Committee, were deeply concerned by the shortages that war would bring. If the enemy could encircle the British Isles, food and other essentials would be in dire shortage, and the country would begin to tear itself apart from within as desperate citizens fought over whatever scraps they could find. NARPAC issued a pamphlet advising people that, if it was impossible to move their beloved pets to the countryside, it would be best to put them down; an advert for a bolt gun was printed next to the information.

Despite protests from animal rights groups such as the RSPCA and PDSA, a panicked population rushed

22

to veterinary centres to have their animals euthanized. In one week, it is believed that as many as 750,000 animals died. Long before the horrors of the final solution were known, this was referred to as the September holocaust. Battersea Dogs' Home managed to save 145,000 dogs from certain death.

What is odd about this incident is the weight of government advice and the panic people must have felt to offer up their pets so quickly. Tragically, with hindsight, the animal cull was clearly unnecessary and years later many pet owners were bitter and angry with the government. Radio broadcaster Christopher Stone stating, 'To destroy a faithful friend when there is no need to do so is yet another way of letting war creep into your home.'

The 2017 book *The Great Dog and Cat Massacre* by Hilda Kean explains this tragic moment of British history in depth.

THE CHANNEL ISLANDS

!

On Sunday 30th June 1940 a German plane circled over Guernsey before landing on the island's airport. The local 'bobby' (policeman) scurried over to the Germans who had landed with a letter from the bailiff, 'This Island has been declared an Open Island by His Majesty's Government of the United Kingdom. There are no armed forces of any description. The bearer has been instructed to hand this communication to you. He does not understand the German language.' And so began the five-year occupation of Britain's Channel Islands, arguably the most lackluster occupation of the entire war. Strategically, the islands were worthless, but the propaganda value of having Britons within the Reich was priceless.

Following the fall of Dunkirk and anticipating invasion, thousands of islanders had already evacuated to the mainland. Boats were made ready to take as many to England as possible. Not all could, or would, leave. Among them were a handful of Jews, twelve on Jersey and four on Guernsey.

Despite Churchill's roared speeches of defiance, there was no fighting on the beaches, the streets or the hills. People got on with their lives, just as did the men and women of any occupied country, trying to maintain the fine line between independence and normality without crossing it and risking German reprisals. The British were treated gently compared to other nations, perhaps as an experiment in appeasing the British so they would listen to Hitler's 'appeal to reason' and make peace, or a taste of things to come if Britain was invaded and Operation Sea Lion worked?

Radios were confiscated, phone lines cut, spirits and petrol were banned, permits were needed for boats and an 11pm – 6am curfew was put in place. Eddie Chapman, one of the most enigmatic men of the war, was in prison for burglary. He tried to escape prison and was sent to Paris where he offered to work for the Germans as a spy, they accepted his offer. Codenamed *Zig-Zag* by the British and *Fritz* by the Germans, he would eventually become a double agent under Cecil Masterman's XX Committee. He is the only Englishman to have received the Iron Cross.

In April 1942 three Jewish women on Guernsey, Therese Steiner, Marianne Grunfeld and Auguste Spitz were in trouble. The British bobbies told the women to pack their bags and report to the police station, where they'd be handed over to the German military the next day, last stop, Auschwitz.

What is upsetting here is the absolute compliance of the police. It is no secret that the horror show of the holocaust was only possible because of the never-ending army of myrmidons who were 'just following orders'. Was there really no opportunity to give the women a heads-up? There was a whole evening of waiting – could the women not have 'escaped' police custody and found an old boat on the shore?

Police Clerk Sergeant Ernest Plevin gave an absolutely scandalous justification for the complicity of the British police: 'Police involvement in deportations was rarely more than carrying out orders given by the occupying forces.' (What else would it be!)

A 1945 British intelligence report was deeply concerned by the actions of the islands police and local authorities. The report laments they put up absolutely no protest to anti-Jewish measures, knowing full well the Jews would receive 'unpleasant' treatment in Europe. In contrast, the islanders did everything possible to protect Freemasons. Women who fraternized with occupying soldiers became known as 'Jerry-bags'; estimates for the number of illegitimate children from these relationships ranged from 80 – 900. Wretched slave labourers skulking around the island, of whom 700 died, would have brought the horrors of the Reich home to the locals. With all this being said, it was easy for mainlanders who weren't in danger (and modern minds) to condemn and judge when they have never been in such an excruciating position themselves. The majority of Channel Islanders acted stoically and honourably in extremely difficult circumstances.

Photographs of German soldiers parading through the streets, chatting happily to the local bobby, and perusing shops with English signage still shock and fascinate today.

CAMP E715

!!

The unbelievable horrors that emerged from the string of concentration camps across Europe is well documented: millions of Jews, disabled people, political dissidents, prisoners of war, and other 'undesirables', suffered to such an extreme that, despite overwhelming evidence, a minority today still cannot – or refuse to – believe it was real.

One of the lesser-known stories is that of Arthur Dodd, a British soldier in the Royal Army Service Corps. Dodd was captured by the enemy at Badir during the Desert War and ended up in several Italian Prisoner of War camps. In 1943 he was transferred to Auschwitz III (Monowitz), a slave labour site for the pharmaceutical giant IG Farben just five miles away from the infamous Auschwitz-Birkenau site.

The horror of this place became apparent immediately to Dodd. As he and his comrades disembarked from the train they were greeted by the site of an SS officer thrashing a topless teenage Jewish girl with a whip. They tried to intervene but the SS officer pulled out a pistol, a Wehrmacht soldier warned them the SS would have no qualms about killing anyone. Leaving the British with no choice but to let the thrashing continue.

Dodd's home for the next 14 months was camp E715, close enough to the crematoria for the smell of burning flesh to fill the air, bodies hung from gallows and the men witnessed the unbelievable treatment of the inmates, particularly the Jews. Some of the men tried to sneak food to the other inmates, but others refused to help, openly admitting they believed that anyone being treated as cruelly as the Jews of Auschwitz were obviously being punished for a crime they had committed of equal ferocity.

Opportunities for defiance were slim, but the soldiers tried. Being forced to work on pipework at Monowitz, the men began to deliberately sabotage them by filling them with stones and other items. A German engineer became suspicious and ordered a test. The men were horrified – their act of sabotage would soon be discovered and the best they could hope for was to be lined up and shot. As the test began, an air raid siren sounded. The men were rushed to an air raid shelter. When they emerged, they discovered the only place that was actually hit by bombs was where their pipes were. All of them were destroyed and their sabotage effort was never discovered.

With the war coming to an end and the Allies closing in, the guards gave Dodd and his men a choice to walk towards the Soviets in the east or the Americans in the west. They choose the westward journey and they were eventually liberated at Regensburg, Germany.

After the war, Dodd returned to Britain, marrying his sweetheart Olwen and starting a family. His account of his time in the war, *Spectator in Hell*, was published in 1998.

CHANSON D'AUTOMNE

!!!

C hanson d'automne (Autumn song) is one of the most famous French poems. Written by Paul Verlaine around 1866, it was part of his 'sad landscapes' collection.

The long tears
Of Autumn's
Violins
Wound my heart
With a monotonous
Lethargy.

All suffocating
And pale when
The hour strikes
I remember
The old days
And I cry…

And I am going away
On an ill wind

> That carries me
> Here, there,
> Just like a
> Dead leaf.

This poem would do its bit for the war effort nearly eighty years later. The British, through the BBC radio broadcasts, would give the nod to the French Resistance that the time for Operation Overlord and the D-Day landings were almost at hand.

The first three lines of the poem, when played on the radio, would secretly inform the resistance that Operation Overlord was to start within two weeks, these were broadcast on the 1st June 1944. The next set of lines would tell the French that the landings would start within 48 hours, these were broadcast on 5th June at 23:15, the night before D-Day. Such a cunning and clandestine use of a poem was indecipherable to German counterintelligence.

The broadcasts were successful in informing the French Resistance that it was now time to prepare to fight. With the broadcast of this poem they began sabotage operations such as blowing up railways and blocking roads and generally hindered the enemy in any way they could.

CHARLIE BROWN

!

In any war, particularly one as nightmarish and devastating as the Second World War, simple acts of compassion and chivalry stand out. Rare flashes of humanity in the senseless slaughter of war are poignant reminders to us that people can defy the odds. One such incident was between Charlie Brown and Franz Stigler.

Lt. Charlie Brown was a USAAF pilot, commanding a Boeing B-17 Flying Fortress, 'Ye Olde Pub', on a bombing run over Bremen. Brown was flying in left of the formation, known as the 'Purple Heart corner' for its vulnerability. On return from the bombing run, enemy flak and fighters crippled the plane, their compass and engines were damaged and the crew did not know where they were. They could have been flying deeper into the Reich rather than returning to Britain. The tail gunner had been killed and nine other crewmen were injured. The oxygen system was damaged, causing Brown to momentarily black out; he regained consciousness just in time to stop his spiraling plane crashing into the ground.

Franz Stigler, a Luftwaffe ace with 27 victories to his name intercepted the B-17 and couldn't believe it was still airborne in the state it was in. Stigler, risking his own life, flew his Messerschmitt Bf 109 G-6 alongside the plane to see a panicked Charlie Brown and the injured crew desperately trying to make it home. Stigler hoped the plane would land, or at least head towards neutral Sweden. It became clear to Stigler that Brown was determined to reach England. He turned his plane and escorted the bomber back to Britain, accompanying it part of the way across the North Sea. Brown, still not entirely sure of the enemy pilot's intentions, ordered his dorsal turret gunner to aim at the Messerschmitt but not to open fire. Stigler gave Brown a salute and left. 'Ye Olde Pub' eventually made it back to base. The incident concerned Allied command, and the crew were ordered to keep quiet as positive sentiment for the enemy was considered dangerous. Brown himself later commenting 'someone decided you can't be human and flying in a German cockpit.' Stigler kept the incident to himself too, as he risked execution for his insubordination.

Decades after the war, Brown was desperate to track down the man who spared him and his crew. Years of searching revealed nothing until a chance letter to a pilots' newsletter came to the attention of Stigler, who was by then living in Canada. Forty years later the two men were reunited and remained life-long friends, dying a few months apart of each other in 2008.

CHIPS THE DOG

!!

Chips, a mix of a German shepherd, collie and husky served in the United States Army, and is believed to be the most decorated canine of the Second World War. During the war, American families donated their dogs for military service and in 1942 the Wren family offered Chips, who became a sentry dog.

Among his valiant efforts was his part in the 1943 invasion of Sicily. During the assault, Chips, along with his handler Pvt. John Rowell and his men were pinned down by a machine gun nest. The dog broke cover and charged towards the nest, biting enemy soldiers and pulling a smoking machine gun from its base. Chips grabbed one of the enemy by his neck and dragged him out from his cover; the soldier and his comrades surrendered. Later in the day Chips took a further ten Italian soldiers prisoner.

Chips was also given the honour of being a guard at a meeting between Winston Churchill and Franklin D. Roosevelt. He wasn't always well behaved though. When the future president General Dwight D.

Eisenhower went to pet him, he bit him. The fault can't lie completely at Chips door for this incident. He was trained to clamp down on any humans he didn't know.

In December 1945 Chips was reunited with his owners, the Wren family. Sadly, though, he would die just seven months later, probably as a result of complications from injuries he sustained during his service.

In 1990, Disney made a film on the dog's life, *Chips, the War Dog.* In 2018, Chips was posthumously awarded the prestigious Dickin Medal for his heroic actions.

CROFT'S PIKES

!!!

The British Home Guard, the last-ditch call up of old men and those deemed unfit for active service, is considered peculiarly endearing to the British. This is thanks, in part, to the BBC comedy series, *Dad's Army* (1968 – 1977), which followed a group of bumbling and incompetent, but well-meaning and courageous, reservists.

The atmosphere in Britain at the time would not have been light-hearted. The threat of Nazi invasion, through Operation Sea Lion, was considered real, plausible and imminent. The volunteers were to be the last line, holding off *Fallschirmjaeger* (paratroopers) and coastal assaults in the desperate hope of buying the doomed country some time, fighting heroically to the last man. Thankfully, the Home Guard never saw combat, and the events of 1941 turned the tides of war in a different direction. However, they remained on guard, and it was possible, though increasingly unlikely as the war progressed, that the tide could turn once more. Perhaps a reasonably reliable comparison to the heroic desperation and mindset of the Home Guard is the tragic *Volkssturm* (people's storm) of Nazi Germany.

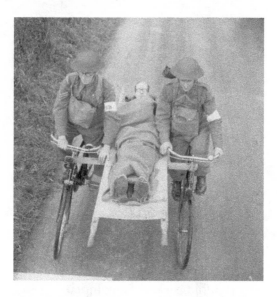

1940 was arguably Britain's most dangerous year – certainly just after the miraculous escape from Dunkirk. 1,682,000 men volunteered for the Home Guard, but there were not enough weapons, 739,000 were unarmed. In 1941, Churchill wrote, possibly tongue-in-cheek, that 'every man must have a weapon of some sort, be it only a mace or pike.' Whether or not Churchill was speaking literally about medieval weapons, he was taken at his word. A quarter of a million pikes were ordered, long steel tubes fixed with a bayonet.

The soldiers of the Home Guard were obviously unimpressed, and it is believed none were issued after protestations. Lord Croft, Under-Secretary of State for War said in the House of Commons, defending the pike, it was 'a most effective and silent weapon'. Others suggest that 'Croft's Pikes' *were* a serious suggestion by Churchill, but Lord Croft did the honourable thing and took the blame away from the Prime Minister for this foible.

The armament crisis was eventually resolved with all the reservists being properly equipped. Quite how the Wehrmacht would have reacted if they invaded Britain, being met on the shores by elderly men with pikes, can only be guessed at. For those who have seen *Dad's Army*, we can imagine the reaction of Captain Mainwaring and his men: 'We're doomed!'

DADA

!!

The First World War destroyed the established order. Millions of men died and were wounded during a seemingly pointless conflict. Throughout Europe, the old order crumbled and extremist groups such as fascists and communists began to fill the void for the survivors of an angry and bitter generation.

Even the arts were affected, an avant-garde movement known as Dada or Dadaism began to emerge from 1916 onwards, as a reaction to the horrors of the Great War itself, and a rejection of bourgeois capitalism, colonialism and other Western constructs. Dada artists enjoyed the absurd, nonsensical and surreal. Although difficult to define, some of its main manifestations were poetry, collages, photomontages and literature.

Dadaism wasn't popular with everyone. *The American Art News* described the movement as 'Dada philosophy is the sickest, most paralyzing and most destructive thing that has ever originated from the brain of man.' Later described as a 'reaction to what many of these artists saw as nothing more than an insane spectacle of collective homicide.' Dadaism spilled over into the Second World War, even being condemned during Goebbels 'degenerate art exhibition' in 1937.

One of the most striking Dada artists was the German John Heartfield. His Anglicised name was his own choice, he changed it from Helmut Herzfeld and was appalled by the anti-British sentiment of the First World War, the cries of 'May God punish England', and the general fervour for bloodshed sweeping Europe. The same 'us vs. them' mob mentality was swirling in Britain.

Heartfield's anti-Nazi photomontages have a strikingly modern feel to them. In different pieces Goering sets fire to the world; a swastika is crafted by four bloody axes; an ape Hitler sits atop the globe in a *stahlhelm*; a starving family gratefully eat a bicycle and Hitler the butcher grins menacingly over a French cockerel.

Unsurprisingly, the Nazis were not happy with Heartfield's work and in 1933 the SS broke into his apartment in the hope of arresting him. Heartfield managed to hide in a rubbish bin, waiting for hours until they left and managed to escape first to Czechoslovakia and, later, Britain. He earned his place as number five on the Gestapo's most-wanted list.

He returned to Germany in 1950, now partitioned into east and west, and narrowly avoided a trial for treason, because of his time in Britain, from the communist East German government.

His work is still popular and referenced. One

example is the modern rock band System of a Down, who used his piece 'The Hand Has Five Fingers', as a cover for their 1998 debut album.

Though not a surrealist painting, Heinrich Vogeler's striking 'The Third Reich' from 1934 is another piece that appears to be before its time. Vogeler was not as lucky as Heartfield. A German who turned communist as a result of what he had experienced during the First World War, he emigrated with his wife to Russia. After the Axis invasion of the Soviet Union in 1941, Vogeler, along with all Germans, was deported to Kazakhstan. He died there in 1942 from illness due to the squalid living conditions he faced. The Heinrich Vogeler Museum was opened in 2004 in Worpswede, Germany.

DEAR HITLER

!!!

Mohandas Gandhi, the Indian revolutionary, is one of the most famous faces in history. His non-violent resistance to British imperialist rule sent shockwaves through the world and helped crumble the last remnants of colonialism. History better remembers him by his honorific title Mahatma (venerable).

In the 1930s, Gandhi was clearly disturbed by the events unfolding in Europe. Two curious letters were written by Gandhi and posted to Hitler.

The first letter of 23 July 1939 reads:

> Dear friend,
>
> Friends have been urging me to write to you for the sake of humanity. But I have resisted their request, because of the feeling that any letter from me would be an impertinence. Something tells me that I must not calculate and that I must make my appeal for whatever

it may be worth. It is quite clear that you are today the one person in the world who can prevent a war which may reduce humanity to the savage state. Must you pay the price for an object however worthy it may appear to you to be? Will you listen to the appeal of one who has deliberately shunned the method of war not without considerable success? Any way I anticipate your forgiveness, if I have erred in writing to you.

I remain,
Your sincere friend
M.K.Gandhi

A second, longer letter in 1940 is a much more direct and imploring than the first. In it, Gandhi demonstrated the values, perhaps somewhat naively given the recipient, of pacifism and non-violent resistance.

The letters never reached Hitler, having been intercepted by the British. Even with this in mind, we must take into account Hitler's appetite for war, the countless appeals for sanity since his rise in 1933 and his views on race and 'sub-humans.' It would be extremely surprising if he had any time to entertain the ideas of a Hindu ascetic, though he did in fact later support the creation of an Indian Waffen-SS unit, led by Subhas Chandra Bose, though this was most likely out of pragmatism.

This tragically optimistic correspondence was dramatized in the 2011 Bollywood movie, *Dear Friend Hitler*.

DEATH RAY

!!!

It was not just the Nazis who had a penchant for wonder weapons, miraculous inventions so powerful they'd change the course of the war and bring all other nations into submission. The Japanese were in on it too, having hopes for a death ray.

Since 1924, some scientists had been boasting of their ability to build a death ray. But it was Nikola Tesla in 1934 who stated in an interview with Time Magazine of the potential of wiping out entire squadrons of planes and armies 250 miles away using 'teleforce.' Tesla made contact with the US military, who weren't particularly interested in his claims – but the article made the Japanese wonder whether it could be done.

After the war, documents confiscated by the US military showed a laboratory in Noborito had been working on this potentially deadly weapon. Development had begun on a device named 'Ku-Go': a large magnetron which created powerful microwaves. It was planned to beam radiation at enemies, killing soldiers and destroying equipment.

Fortunately the project floundered. The end of the war stopped the research.

Unlike the lethal death rays of popular science fiction a decade or so later, the Japanese version was not as dangerous. At the peak of research, a focused beam could kill a rabbit from 1,000 yards away - assuming it would stay still for five minutes.

The British themselves dabbled with the idea of a death ray under the guidance of Sir Henry Tizard, Robert Watkins Watt and other academics before finding it unfeasible. This may have been a blessing in disguise, as they developed the game-changing concept of radar instead.

DESMOND DOSS

!

Desmond Doss was a celebrated hero of the war. Born in Lynchburg, Virginia in 1919 to a Seventh-day Adventist family, the man was deeply religious. His beliefs meant he was classified as a conscientious objector during the war. Refusing to carry a weapon when signing up for the army in April 1942, he assumed he would be trained as a combat medic, only he wasn't.

His initial relationship was tense. His comrades didn't trust a soldier who wouldn't carry a gun. Many of them bullied him and tried to make his life as difficult as possible in the hope of making him leave, breaking his nerve, or even getting him court marshalled, but Doss refused to go. Ultimately, he stuck to his principles and was transferred and became an army medic with the 77th Division.

Despite refusing to kill, in battle Doss earned the respect and admiration of the men for his courage and selflessness. Fighting in the Pacific theatre, he received two Bronze Star medals for exceptional valor in assisting his comrades. He saw action at Guam,

Leyte and Okinawa.

At Okinawa, his division was fighting to take the 350ft high Maeda Escarpment, a rock face known by the Americans as Hacksaw Ridge. After finally securing it, the soldiers were startled by a vicious Japanese counterattack. The fighting was hard and bloody, not all the men managed to escape when the order to retreat was given. Those who could withdraw did so - except Doss. The medic charged back into combat, scurrying among the wounded, dying and dead to save as many lives as he could and carry them to safety. He refused to retreat until every soldier with a chance was away from the fight. As many as 75 soldiers survived thanks to the medic. He did this despite being injured four times in this battle. He was badly wounded by a grenade, and shrapnel tore through his leg. While struggling on, he was hit by a sniper's bullet in the arm. Even after making it to safety, he gave up his litter for another wounded man. He was evacuated on 21st May 1945, aboard the USS *Mercy*.

Doss was one of 431 servicemen to receive the Congressional Medal of Honor. Throughout his life his golden rule, in fact, *the* Golden Rule from many of the world's religions was, 'do to others what you would have them do to you' (Matthew 7:12). Doss died in 2006. Mel Gibson's 2016 movie *Hacksaw Ridge* is based on the man's extraordinary life.

DIE GLOCKE

!!!

Die Glocke (the Bell) was a groundbreaking Nazi invention in the closing stages of the war, supposedly worked on from a secret base in Poland's Wenceslas mines. Die Glocke, one of countless *wunderwaffen* (wonder weapons), allowed its operators to travel into space, using gravity-defying technology to reach as far as the Moon and even Mars. The bell-shaped craft, three metres in diameter, was powered by a secretive 'red mercury' substance. After the war, it was captured by US forces and taken back to America. Observers of the famous 1947 Roswell Incident state the crashed UFO they saw was Die Glocke. It could even manipulate time.

Of course, this is all nonsensical. Despite imaginative conspiracy theories involving Antarctic bases and alien races – the first mention of Die Glocke was actually from 2000, sixty-five years after the war ended. Oh, and there is no substance known as 'red mercury'. We owe our current speculation of Die Glocke to the Polish journalist Igor Witkowski, in his book *Prawda o Wunderwaffe*.

It's likely that Die Glocke was dreamt up from a confused rehash from the 1960 occult book *The Morning of the Magicians* by Louis Pauwels and Jacques Bergier, which thought up similar concoctions. It is believed, in turn, that the *The Morning of the Magicians,* and the subsequent imaginative theories, was actually inspired by the famed science-fiction writer H. P. Lovecraft.

THE DIRLEWANGER BRIGADE

!!

Oskar Dirlewanger is one of those historical caricatures who, if we didn't know he really existed, we could easily assume was fictional - a character from a horribly grim story. Dirlewanger is in this book because his actions were so vile that they were enough to even appall his Nazi comrades in the SS.

He was a veteran of the Great War and had been awarded the Iron Cross for his actions. After the signing of the Treaty of Versailles, he took part in the failed Kapp Putsch of 1920. He joined several *Freikorps*, the brutal paramilitary forces made up of veterans, and joined in the crushing of Communist uprisings that occurred during the interbellum years of the Weimar Republic.

With the rise of Hitler and his *Sturmabteilung*, he saw a cause which matched his own views. He joined the brownshirts in 1932. Two years later, he was convicted of abusing a 14-year-old girl and sentenced to two years in prison. He was released in time to take part in the Spanish civil war, as part of Germany's Condor Legion.

Dirlewanger appealed personally to Heinrich Himmler to join the Waffen-SS, and thanks to friends in high places his wish was granted. Obersturmfuhrer Dirlewanger was even given command of his own unit, which was named after him.

The Dirlewanger Brigade was, at first, made up of 'honourable poachers' -- those convicted for poaching, whose invaluable skills in the wild and flouting of the law would make them ideally suited for the unit. Over time convicted prisoners from all walks of life would join up as an alternative to prison to 'redeem' themselves in the eyes of the Reich. The SS, with their bizarrely paradoxical code of honour, were disgusted by the unit.

Dirlewanger and his men were in their element fighting 'bandits', usually unarmed civilians far from the battlefront. Rape, looting, indiscriminate slaughter and general terrorizing of the local population, often while drunk, was where this unit excelled. One such 'anti-partisan' action reported 386 'bandits dead' and, an ominously vague, 294 'bandit suspects finished off'.

The SS proper, for reasons best known to themselves given their own actions, were outraged by this unit. They sought to put Dirlewanger on trial to answer for his crimes, but friends in high places made sure this didn't happen.

The unit took part in crushing the Warsaw Uprising, joined by Ukrainians and Cossacks. They went house-to-house, slaughtering those within, and murdering the patients of a hospital. The nurses who survived were sent, naked and bleeding, running into the streets.

With the vengeful Red Army pouring towards Germany, Dirlewanger's men were forced to fight at the front. Fighting actual soldiers was something they were pitifully inadequate at, and the unit crumbled in the face of resistance. Many deserted or defected, and the unit all but ceased to exist. Dirlewanger himself was injured and removed from the front, vanishing soon afterwards.

He was arrested on 1st June 1945 under a fake identity while hiding in a remote hunting lodge. While interned, he was recognized by concentration camp survivors. Within a few days he was dead, officially of 'natural causes.' Some say he was beaten to death by Polish camp guards, others that he escaped and took part in all sorts of imaginative escapades. Authorities dug up his body in 1960 to put that nonsense to bed once and for all.

THE EXORCIST

!!

In 2006, Father Gabriel Amorth, an official exorcist for the Vatican, announced to the world that Hitler and Stalin were possessed. During the radio interview Amorth explained that the men were under the influence of the devil.

As a result, Pope Pius XII (Eugenio Pacelli) during the war, attempted a 'long distance' exorcism of the brutal dictators; Amorth explained why this didn't work.

'It's very rare that praying and attempting to carry out an exorcism from a distance work. Of course you can pray for someone from a distance but in this case it would not have any effect. One of the key requirements of an exorcism is to be present in front of the possessed person and that person also has to be consenting and willing... However I have no doubt that Hitler was possessed and so it does not surprise me that Pope Pius XII tried a long distance exorcism.'

However, Amorth also believed wholeheartedly in the satanic evil of Harry Potter and yoga. His favourite film was *The Exorcist*, which he thought was accurate but a bit heavy handed on the special effects...

FACES OF THE REICH

!!

Werner Goldberg is one of the most famous faces from the war years. He was born in Konigsberg, Germany, in 1919. Later in his life his uncle became a zealous member of the nascent Nazi party. In 1938, Goldberg joined the Reich Labour Service, and by September 1939 he was a soldier taking part in the invasion of Poland.

Goldberg was handsome, and he was astonished to find that his official military photograph had been sold by the *Heer*, the German army, to the *Berliner Tagesblatt* newspaper. He was described as 'the perfect German soldier' and his *stahlhelm* adorned head was soon being used for recruitment posters throughout the country.

There was just one little issue with the Reich's new golden boy; he was half-Jewish. Goldberg was a 'first-degree *mischling*' in the parlance of the Nazi justice system. In 1940 he was dismissed from the *Wehrmacht*, as were all 'first-degree' *mischling*, on Hitler's orders, and spent five dangerous years trying to stay alive. Goldberg and his father were the only members of his family to survive the war. Goldberg himself died in Berlin in 2004.

That wasn't the end of the debacle though. In 2015 a Russian war monument in Tobolsk to the 'defenders of the motherland for all time' bizarrely, somehow, used Goldberg's face for the etching! This was later changed.

The embarrassing foibles kept coming. *Sonne ins Haus* (Sun in the Home) was a Nazi-backed magazine. A 1935 edition features a cute 'Aryan' baby wearing a bonnet on the front cover. The face of this shining example of Aryan youth was, naturally, a Jewish girl named Hessy Levinsons Taft.

Taft's parents, Jacob and Pauline, had taken her to have a photograph taken when she was a year old, as most parents would who could afford it, and thought nothing more of it. But they were later astonished to find their baby daughter's photograph on the cover of the magazine, the winner of a competition hand-picked by Joseph Goebbels! The parents were horrified and contacted the photographer, telling him they were Jewish. The photographer admitted he knew. He discovered Goebbel's beautiful Aryan baby competition, and surreptitiously entered Taft's photograph to mock it and 'make the Nazis ridiculous'.

The Nazis never uncovered the truth. The family was able to escape Germany, eventually ending up in the United States. This story came to the world's attention in 2014 when Taft donated the *Sonne ins Haus* magazine to *Yad Vashem*, the World Holocaust Remembrance Centre.

FIFTH SYMPHONY

!!

'V for Victory' became one of the most famous and enduring symbols of resistance to Nazi occupation throughout the war. Vs and V graffiti were plastered everywhere. Colonel Britton, the voice of the European service called for people to 'Splash the V from one end of Europe to another.' Colonel Britton was in fact Douglas Ritchie, an assistant news editor at the BBC, whose identity was a closely guarded secret until the end of the war.

It dawned on Ritchie that the four opening notes of Beethoven's fifth symphony were extremely similar to the Morse code for V (dot-dot-dot-dash). It became his theme song and listeners copied the sound however they could.

This piece is further fitting when you consider that Beethoven was German, and gradually went deaf. He used the vibrations of sound to understand music. Of his fifth symphony being a symbol of resistance, it was said by Victor de Laveleye, a Belgian exile broadcasting from London, that the theme would remind the enemy that they were 'surrounded, encircled by an immense crowd of citizens eagerly awaiting his first moment of weakness, watching for his first failure.'

FIRE HEDGEHOG

!!

There were many weird and wacky technological inventions put forward during the war. A Soviet contribution to this was the Fire Hedgehog. 88 PPSh-41 submachine guns were strapped into the bomb bay of a modified Tupolev Tu-2 aircraft giving the impression of the needles of a curled up hedgehog. Upon approaching a concentration of enemy forces, the bomb bays would open and let rip a salvo of 7.62mm bullets.

It is unclear whether the weapon was ever used, and if so to what effect. But in principle – despite running out of ammunition in five seconds – the weapon could be devastating to a concentration of people on the ground.

Like most of the weird and wonderful weapons of the war, it was not so much whether the concept was effective, but simply that research and development was focused onto more resourceful and tried and tested ideas.

FLIGHT 19

!!

December 5th 1945, five Grumman TBM Avengers led by Commander Charles Taylor took off from their naval base at Fort Lauderdale, Florida. They never returned. The US Navy's report on this mystery said that their disappearance on that clear day was for 'reasons unknown': the legend of the lost patrol was born.

The training exercise in which they vanished involved flying 56 miles east into the Atlantic to practice bombing. They should then have travelled east a further 67 miles, in the direction of the Bahamas, before turning north for 73 miles and finally completing their triangular route by flying 120 miles back to base. Upon losing contact, a Martin PBM Mariner was deployed to find them. This did not return either.

The exact cause of their disappearance remains a mystery, though experts generally agree it was down to a faulty compass, a lack of navigational training, or the incompetence of Taylor.

Flight 19 would come to contribute greatly to the

legend of the Bermuda Triangle, or 'the Devil's Triangle', in which countless planes and ships would disappear. Experts have dismissed claims that there is anything odd about an arbitrary triangle stretching roughly between Florida, Bermuda and Puerto Rico. Although there have, of course, been disappearances, considering the sheer volume of traffic in the area, the triangle does not have a peculiar number of incidents. Others have stuck to their guns, claiming that there is a disproportionate number of unexplained events, with some even suggesting that the Bermuda Triangle is proof of extraterrestrial activity, while others equally rationally blame the lost island of Atlantis.

FUEHRER GLOBE

!

Hitler's Globe, officially the Columbus Globe for State and Industry Leaders, was one of two globes (or more, depending on the source) made specifically for him, the other being made for the Nazi party as a whole. Made in the 30s, this globe would have probably been of little interest to people, until Charlie Chaplin's 1940 film *The Great Dictator* lampooned him and his possession. This film was controversial, for although Chaplin was an Englishman, the film was American and the United States were at that time neutral.

A famous part of the film sees Chaplin portraying Adenoid Hynkel, leader of Tomainia, and is clearly based on Hitler, silently playing with the globe, fawning over it and gently dancing with it, as if the whole world was his. The globe eventually bursts and Hynkel is heartbroken.

Reported to be almost as big as a car, Hitler's Globe moved with the Nazis from their old Reich Chancellery to the new one, where it remained until the Soviets arrived in April 1945.

One globe, which allegedly belonged to the dictator, was taken from the 'Eagle's Nest' in Berchtesgaden by the American John Barsamia. His loot returned with him to America, where he kept it for sixty years. When it was sold at a San Francisco auction in 2007 it reached $100,000. As for *the* globe, its fate is unknown.

What is as mysterious as the disappearance of the globe itself, are the countless conspiracy theories regarding its whereabouts. It doesn't seem that Hitler had any particular fondness for it, and why this single item has become so notorious, lying at the centre of some truly outlandish claims, and holding such a fascination for so many conspiracy theorists, is unclear.

GELI RAUBAL

!!

G eli Raubal was born on the 4th June 1908, the daughter of Leo and Angela, Hitler's half-sister. When Angela became widowed in 1928, Hitler invited her to become a housekeeper at his residence, the Berghof in Obersalzburg. Her daughter came with her. Geli would move into Hitler's Munich apartment with him the following year.

All evidence suggests Hitler became infatuated his niece, stating: 'a girl of eighteen to twenty is as malleable as wax. It should be possible for a man, whoever the chosen woman may be, to stamp his own imprint on her. That's all the woman asks for.' According to Patrick Hitler, his American nephew, Geli affectionately called him 'Uncle Alf.'

As Hitler rose to power, he would often bring Geli with him. Her presence was a surprise to the high ranking officials at the solemn meetings he was attending. Ian Kershaw, the English historian, has noted 'for the first time in his life (if we leave his mother out of consideration) he became emotionally dependent on a woman.' Hitler became possessive of his new pet, dismissing his personal chauffeur Emil Maurice, upon discovering the two were having a relationship. Maurice was an early Nazi stalwart, having joined in the Beer Hall Putsch and having been incarcerated alongside the future Fuehrer in Landsberg Prison. The jealousy was mutual. Geli was herself troubled by a seventeen-year-old girl called Eva Braun who had recently caught Hitler's eye.

Geli Raubal gradually became little more than a prisoner. Her hopes of escaping to Vienna, the site of Hitler's failed art career, were dashed when he forbade it. On 18th September 1931 there was a heated argument between them. He was informed the next day that his niece had shot herself with his Walther pistol, though it was said that an optimistic hand-written letter was left unfinished on her writing desk.

Hitler was devastated with the turn of events, declaring she was the only woman he had ever loved. Afterwards her Obersalzburg room was left untouched, and a portrait of the doomed girl hung at the Chancellery in Berlin.

Countless speculations have arisen since the event. Local papers and political opponents scandalised the story, and there have been theories bandied about involving pregnancy, murder and violence. An SA officer, Wilhelm Stocker, claimed many years later that '[Geli] admitted to me that at times Hitler made her do things in the privacy of her room that sickened her, but when I asked her why she didn't refuse to do them, she just shrugged and said that she didn't want to lose him to some woman who would do what he wanted.' Though such defamatory allegations must be taken with a very large pinch of salt.

A coincidence worth noting now is that of Bernhard Stempfle, a Catholic priest, die-hard Nazi, and alleged co-author of *Mein Kampf*. Despite being one of Hitler's inner circle, he mysteriously fell out of favour with him, being deported to Dachau concentration camp, and then murdered in the woods. It is widely believed that Stempfle knew too much about the Fuehrer's past and personal life.

Whatever the truth of it, Geli Raubal's death was quickly covered up and any hope of knowing what really happened during this enigmatic episode is now lost.

G.I. JOE

!!

Many grown-up boys may remember having owned at least one or two G.I. Joes from when they were children (Action Men in the UK). The manly action figures with their various uniforms and weapons and flicking eyes have been popular for decades. However, their namesake was a hero of a completely different caliber.

In October 1943, the invasion of Italy was raging as the Western Allies fought to establish footholds on the continent. The British 56th London Infantry Division had taken the village of Calvi Vecchia. But their capture of the village was unreported. In the midst of the chaos and confusion of battle, air support had been requested to bomb the village. It was believed that the enemy was still defending it. The only hope for the villagers and the British soldiers alike was GI Joe, a pigeon. Taking the urgent message, Joe set off for the air base and managed to cover twenty miles in an incredible twenty minutes! The message to call off the attack arrived just in time, because the bombers were preparing to launch. It is estimated that Joe saved over 1,000 lives that day.

Joe retired after the war, with 24 of his pigeon comrades to Fort Monmouth in New Jersey. In 1946 he was awarded the Dickin Medal for gallantry, his citation stating '*the most outstanding flight made by a United States Army homing pigeon in World War II.*' He was the first recipient of the Dickin Medal who was not British.

GLASMINE 43

!

War has always given a spur to technological advancement. Soldiers fight, politicians talk, nurses heal; but their success ultimately comes down to the boffins on their side. On a very basic and oversimplified level, it's boiled down to the evolution of oneupmanship. In ancient times cavalry could smash infantry, so spears were developed to stop cavalry; spearmen controlled battlefields, so archers were used to break up their ranks, and so on. Originally this was thanks to the efforts of smiths and armourers, latterly engineers and technicians evolved to take over the new concepts.

So it continued into World War 2. The war that began with the use of horses, biplanes and rifles, would, after only six years, end with tanks, jets and atomic weapons.

A useful means of denying territory to soldiers was the land mine. But land mines were becoming increasingly easy to deal with, using metal detectors and flailing chains on the front of tanks, so this too had to be countered.

The answer was the Glasmine 43, a mine housed in glass. Not only would this be undetectable, but it has the benefit of saving on precious metal, which was needed elsewhere. Glasmine 43 was effective because it was relatively simple: a glass jar containing *Sprengkörper 28*, a 200 gram explosive, atop which a lighter is placed, beneath a pressure plate. When the pressure plate was depressed, the plate broke the igniter and set off the explosion.

Eleven million of these mines were laid throughout the war. Many remain undetected in the ground to this day, such as at Vogelsang Military Training Area. Conflicts of today involve cyber-attacks, drone strikes and use of disinformation. Where it will go next can only be guessed at.

GREMLINS

!!!

Many of us may know of Gremlins because of Joe Dante's 1984 movie, but they were around long before then. They were even said to be involved in World War Two, generally causing mischief and being a nuisance.

During the war, British pilots began to complain of tiny creatures, referred to as gremlins, with a knack for planes, causing aircraft malfunctions, errors, faults and all sorts of headaches. During the Battle of Britain, there were so many reports of these creatures causing plane problems that the Air Ministry put serious time and effort into investigating the phenomena. Workplace posters were put up, advising employees of the various dangers gremlins were apparently involved with. Germans and American pilots later became their victims too. Many crewmen swore blindly they even saw them, menacingly clambering over cockpits or sitting on wingtips.

American aviator Charles Lindberg, in his 1953 book *Spirit of St. Louis* said he met them while flying. He wrote that he was surrounded by several of the creatures, and he was amazed by their advanced technological knowledge. Luckily for Lindberg, he stated these gremlins were friendly, helped him, and reassured him he'd be fine.

Our modern notion of gremlins is thanks to famous children's author Roald Dahl. Dahl himself had served in the RAF and believed he had also been a victim of the gremlins funny business. His book *The Gremlins* was published in 1943 for Walt Disney.

So what was all this about? It must have been a combination of hallucinations caused by the planes high altitudes and the stress of combat that lead to such imaginative scamps.

Perhaps the gremlins were helping in ways the pilots couldn't fathom. By taking the blame for the countless technical issues a pilot faced, the blame was diverted away from the army of factory workers, technicians and engineers who may have actually been at fault.

HAKENKREUZ

!

The swastika remains, perhaps forever, as a symbol of terror and oppression. All of the values of order, law and authority twisted and gnarled into something grotesque and nightmarish. The sight of the swastika, even after all these years, gives us the mental image of Hitler, his legions and all their odious apparatus. But we must, if we can, at least try to remember that the symbol is much older and more powerful than Nazi Germany.

The word swastika itself comes from the Sanskrit word, roughly translating as 'good luck' and is over 7,000 years old. The English first began to use the word in the 1870s.

The peculiarity of this symbol is the contrasting use of it in East and West. In the West, for all obvious reasons, the swastika is now anathema – even today it is still illegal to display it in Germany and several other countries. In the East however, it remains to this day a force for good and a sign of auspiciousness. It is sacred to Hinduism, Buddhism and Jainism.

German archaeologist Henrich Schliemann found

the symbol at the sight of the ancient city of Troy. Schliemann was taken by the symbol, and over time it was slowly transformed into a symbol of 'remote ancestors', the so-called Aryans, and the pseudo-history and unscientific absurdity poured forth from there.

The symbol *was* sacred in the West, and believed to be closely associated with the Viking god Thor, or perhaps Odin, the All-father. But Hitler's use of it, and the SS's use of 'Nordic runes' (actually made up by the nonsensical new-age mystic Guido von List around 1908), has nothing at all to do with the untainted earlier historic period.

The swastika, known as the hakenkreuz (hooked cross) in German was destined to become the symbol of the Nazis. Hitler himself designed the red and white flag on which the hooked cross would sit. 1935 was the year Hitler's standard became the official flag of Germany.

Many academics and authors were appalled by the bizarre appropriation of this ancient symbol. One notable example was Rudyard Kipling. He loved the swastika and many of his books featured them, before the Nazis sullied it. Another was J. R. R. Tolkien, himself of German descent, who was disgusted by the blatant distortion and twisting of Germanic folklore. A planned 1938 German translation of *The Hobbit* was halted when Tolkien was dismayed to receive a letter from the publishers, asking him to prove his Aryan ancestry. It wouldn't reach Germany until 1957. Tolkien described Hitler as a 'ruddy little ignoramus' and was generally disgusted by the whole insanity of the conflict, referring to those who designed as the atomic bomb and bought the war to a cataclysmic end as 'lunatic physicists'.

The symbol was also beloved by the Native Americans. In 1940, four tribes from Arizona officially renounced the symbol in response to the link with Nazi aggression.

With all this in mind, the symbol remains benevolent in the East, and Western misunderstandings of its usage has led to countless protestations and outrages. As an example, an unbelievably ludicrous article from *The Daily Telegraph* in 2017 featured an elderly man who was outraged that the design of the soles of his imported slippers looked a bit like swastikas (they didn't). 2005 saw Prince Harry give the tabloids front-page fodder when he dressed as a Nazi for a fancy-dress party.

One question remains: can the West ever reclaim the ancient swastika, and look beyond its brief abduction as a symbol of evil? And if it can, should it? Or should it belong to the histories, as a stark reminder and warning of the shadow of the past? Perhaps this is a question best left to the sages and scholars among us.

HITLER THE INVINCIBLE

!!

Adolf Hitler believed he was guided by divine providence, being nudged along like a 'sleepwalker' by a higher power that was protecting him. Winston Churchill had a similar line of thought for himself – he had his own experiences that shaped his worldview, and he would even be ordained into the Ancient Order of Druids.

With a figure as controversial and divisive as Hitler, it was not odd that he was the target of multiple assassination attempts. What is odd, bearing in mind how many of them there were, is that all of them failed.

There are too many to list here, and whole books have been written on this subject, but it is believed the dictator survived over thirty plots from the 1930s up unto 1944. Living through every one of these increased the man's paranoia and suspicion, but also cemented his belief in divine providence – surely one must have the favour of the gods to dodge death so many times?

All the attempts failed; lone gunmen, the German military, Poles, the NKVD and the SOE. Many more ideas didn't get past the planning stage, such as the odd plan to return the imprisoned Rudolf Hess to Germany, hypnotized, to finish off his leader! Perhaps the most well-known of these plots was the July 20 plot, where Claus von Stauffenberg and his Wehrmacht conspirators attempted to blow up Hitler during a meeting. This would have probably worked if it wasn't for a last minute change of venue, and the suitcase containing the explosive being accidentally kicked away. This close call was made famous by the 2008 film *Valkyrie* starring Tom Cruise. The bomb detonated, Hitler escaped with a shattered eardrum and a few other minor injuries. He was furious and his vengeance was swift, decimating swathes of German commanders in response.

Interestingly, the British didn't particularly want him dead – the reason for this is that in his final years Hitler was so incompetent and was making such disastrous military decisions that they feared him being replaced by someone more cunning and competent who could lengthen the conflict. Then, of course, there is the glaringly obvious reason not to have killed him before the end of the war. If he *did* die before the war's end, he could have become a martyr. In a similar vein to the stab-in-the-back myth of World War One, fanatical elements might have fought even more fiercely, convinced that Hitler somehow would have turned the tide once more if he was alive. No doubt we would still be bombarded in this day and age with lurid conspiracy theories.

Mussolini and his mistress had been humiliatingly hanged from an Esso petrol station on 28th April 1945 and no doubt a similar fate awaited Hitler. Deep within Berlin's *Fuehrerbunker*, he decided to end his own life. His wife of one day, Eva Braun, joined him by taking a cyanide pill. Hitler probably shot himself. With a twist worthy of *Macbeth*, the dictator who it seemed no living man could kill, finally died on 30th April 1945 by his own hand.

The Soviets soon conquered the *Fuehrerbunker* and this is where things get murky. Stalin, for reasons best known to him, stated that Hitler hadn't died there and was being sheltered by the Allies in Spain or South America – despite overwhelming evidence to the contrary. Experts believe this was done as part of a state sponsored disinformation campaign. But it is unclear what Stalin would have got out of it. Perhaps he genuinely believed it, perhaps he was trying to stir up distrust of the capitalists and imperialists whose temporary alliance with him would soon be severed.

Stalin's response has not helped historians. Theories of Hitler's survival have lived on, growing and exaggerating in the telling. He could be in Spain; more reckon Argentina is a more obvious choice; even a secret Antarctic base has been bandied about - and it's said that he's still alive.

Not bad for a man over 120 years of age!

HOLMAN PROJECTOR

!!!

The Holman Projector was an anti-aircraft weapon used by many British ships and was an impressive piece of improvisation. Several different designs were made but they followed similar lines. It was designed by a machine tool manufacturer, Holmans. A 4' 6" barrel would hold a tin. Inside the tin was a bomb. The bomb's safety pin was held in place by the tin until the bomb was in the air. The weapon used compressed air or high pressure steam to fire the projectile at the enemy. It's main advantage being it was very cheap to build and easy to install.

It was intended to assist the Royal Navy and the Merchant Navy, who were being terrorized by German air attacks during their crucial supply runs. The idea being the bombs could, at the very least, deter low flying attackers and force them to climb to higher altitudes where their attacks would be less accurate.

As an effective anti-aircraft weapon, the Holman Projector was a failure, though one ship did in fact shoot down two enemy planes with it. Its limited range of around 200 yards made it nearly impossible to hit enemy aircraft. A test demonstrating the weapon, witnessed by Winston Churchill, failed because the testers forgot to bring any ammunition! The men improvised and fired off some beer bottles, and an amused Churchill quipped that it would at least 'save on cordite'.

However, as a source of amusement for its users, it was invaluable. As the barrels were smooth-bore, they could be filled with anything. Curious gunners found potatoes were particularly good missiles to fire. Nearby vessels even conducted play fights with them!

HUMAN TROPHIES

!!

It reads like the stuff of nightmares and has been interwoven with fiction and urban legends for centuries: the taking of human trophies. American GIs in the Second World War had a particular contempt for the Japanese: they were the aggressors, and perceived as a brutal, savage and barbaric race. Fighting with the Japanese was always fierce, and the loss of friends and comrades would have further demonized the enemy. Old-fashioned ideas and propaganda portrayed this particular enemy as sub-human. Tragically, this led to a similar attitude to that which saw to the obliteration of the native Americans.

It was claimed many years after the war, when the bodies of Japanese soldiers were repatriated from the Mariana Islands, that half came back without their heads. We should always tread lightly with stories such as this, but it was said that GIs would decapitate enemy corpses and boil the heads until only the skulls remained. They would then use the skulls as camp decorations or ashtrays or have them sent home as trophies. Teeth, arm bones and ears were also popular souvenirs.

The Japanese were outraged when a letter-opener made from a soldier's arm bone was given to President Roosevelt as a present. The US authorities eventually stepped in to stop this macabre practice, ruling that the taking of skulls was in violation of the Geneva Convention.

There is photographic evidence that this gruesome practice occurred but, just as tales of the crimes of Axis soldiers were inflated so that the truth of their actual offences became blurred, the scale of this dark chapter in American history, and the degree of involvement of those alleged to have participated, is unclear.

Experts today believe that acts of cruelty and inhumanity may flourish in any quarter of the globe, when authorities demonise specific demographics and distance themselves from groups considered 'other'. Consequently group-punishment and arbitrary revenge may become tolerated.

INSTRUCTIONS FOR SERVICEMEN

!

The Germans have pleasant beer and excellent sausages, but they are a people prone to hysterical fits if they don't get their own way. Attractive women might be spies, and the rest are generally big, fleshy and fair-haired. Give instructions to them in a firm, military manner – they're used to it and some of them are already planning World War 3. Oh, and the Schnapps is to die for.

This is some of the 'advice' given to the British army in a pamphlet issued to them in 1944 by the Foreign Office, *Instructions for British Servicemen in Germany*. The book is a practical guide to soldiers advising them how to, and how not to, behave when in the country. The book assumes the final victory of the Allies and some of the advice is sound, some accidentally hilarious, and some is clumsily and crudely stereotypical.

Equally fascinating is *Instructions for American Servicemen in Britain* (1942). This advice includes reminding US readers the British aren't the Redcoats of 1776. The Brits like their privacy and don't enjoy small talk. The American and British versions of the English language are very different, colloquialisms and phrases may not translate, their bum is a backside, for example, so be careful not to create any 'boners'. The Brits are fiercely proud of their odd system of pounds, shillings and pence – they don't understand the superior decimal system - so don't mock their 'funny money'. The British are also bitter about being paid much less than GIs, so don't rub it in. Remember the British, despite their reserved nature, are tough. After all, the English empire and its language weren't spread around the world by a bunch of 'panty-waists'.

Both these books and others are a charming glimpse into the past. The *Instructions for British Servicemen in Germany* pamphlet became a best seller in Germany when the Bodleian Library republished it as a book in 2007.

Perhaps some of the messages in these books still ring true, such as the advice 'be firm and just, but don't be soft'.

JANIS PINUPS

!!!

Janis Pinups was the last of the Forest Brothers, an underground resistance movement in the Baltic states, to come out of hiding. During the war the Baltic states had been placed in a unique position: they were conquered by the Soviet Union as part of the Molotov-Ribbentrop Pact, were then invaded by the Axis as part of Operation Barbarossa, were then retaken by the Soviet Union as the Germans were forced to retreat, and remained occupied – without any substantial Allied opposition – until 1991.

Pinups, a native of Latvia, was conscripted into the Red Army in 1944. He was knocked unconscious during a battle, and upon waking, found the battlefield abandoned, and no sign of his comrades. Pinups, a devout Christian, believed God had saved him.

The price of desertion was death and Stalin even punished his soldiers who had surrendered during the war with further imprisonment when they returned home. So Janis Pinups would spend the next fifty years in hiding from the Red Army, living in the wild and an underground bunker. Only his siblings knew he was alive, helping them on their farms under cover of night. Over the long years, his brothers died and he had to stop visiting his sister after neighbours became suspicious of the stranger visiting the farm at impolite hours.

Latvia gained independence in 1991, but the Soviet military continued to have a presence in the country. It was only in 1995, after fifty years, that Pinups surrendered himself to local police. He moved in with his sister until his death in 2007.

JOHN R. MCKINNEY

!

John R. McKinney was an American soldier whose exploits read like the stuff of Hollywood action heroes. He single-handedly fought off 100 Japanese troops during the Philippines campaign.

The citation of his Medal of Honor, which was awarded to him by Harry S. Truman in 1946, read as follows:

'He fought with extreme gallantry to defend the outpost which had been established near Dingalan Bay. Just before daybreak approximately 100 Japanese stealthily attacked the perimeter defense, concentrating on a light machinegun position manned by three Americans. Having completed a long tour of duty at his gun, Pvt. McKinney was resting a few paces away when an enemy soldier dealt him a glancing blow on the head with a saber. Although dazed by the stroke, he seized his rifle, bludgeoned his attacker, and then shot another assailant who was charging him.

Meanwhile, one of his comrades at the machinegun had been wounded and his other companion withdrew carrying the injured man to safety. Alone, Pvt. McKinney was confronted by ten infantrymen who had captured the machinegun with the evident intent of reversing it to fire into the perimeter.

Leaping into the emplacement, he shot seven of them at pointblank range and killed three more with his rifle butt. In the melee the machinegun was rendered inoperative, leaving him only his rifle with which to meet the advancing Japanese, who hurled grenades and directed knee mortar shells into the perimeter. He warily changed position, secured more ammunition, and reloading repeatedly, cut down waves of the fanatical enemy with devastating fire or clubbed them to death in hand-to-hand combat.

When assistance arrived, he had thwarted the assault and was in complete control of the area. Thirty-eight dead Japanese around the machinegun and two more at the side of a mortar 45 yards distant was the amazing toll he had exacted single-handedly.

By his indomitable spirit, extraordinary fighting ability, and unwavering courage in the face of tremendous odds, Pvt. McKinney saved his company from possible annihilation and set an example of unsurpassed intrepidity.'

McKinney died in 1997, and it remains a mystery why Hollywood has not snapped up his incredible story.

JUDY THE DOG

!!

Judy the Pointer was born in the Chinese city of Shanghai in 1936. She escaped from her kennels and lived on the streets for half a year until an incident with Japanese sailors meant she was returned home.

Later that year crew of the gunboat *HMS Gnat* bought Judy, with the dog becoming the ship's mascot. Life aboard the vessel was not always plain-sailing. The Chinese cooks didn't take to her, and her falling out of the boat and being rescued had to be covered up as a training exercise. Judy broke the heart of the mascot for *HMS Ladybird*, a male, as his feelings for her were not reciprocated.

Despite these hiccups, Judy proved herself countless times as an invaluable member of the crew. She alerted the sailors to an impending pirate attack, could hear enemy aircraft before her human shipmates to warn them of the danger, and saved Chief Petty Officer Charles Jeffery from a leopard.

She was married to a French pointer named Paul, who was serving on the gunboat *Francis Garnier*. A wedding celebration was held in Hankou, and after the consummation with Paul, the French Pointer, Judy became pregnant.

With the outbreak of war in 1939, Judy and many crewmates were transferred to *HMS Grasshopper*. This vessel was sunk in the South China Sea in 1942 after being attacked by Japanese aircraft. Judy was saved from the wreckage and the crew ended up on an uninhabited island. Always useful, she dug out a freshwater spring for her comrades, an act which the crew stated saved their lives. Leonard Walter Williams, a British seaman said, 'Judy was a saviour then. She was a marvellous life-saver.'

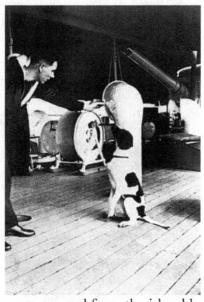

The group were rescued from the island by a Chinese junk. From there, they trekked hundreds of miles towards Padang in Sumatra, but could not be evacuated before the arrival of the Japanese army. On 18th March, they were taken as prisoners of war. Judy became the only recorded canine POW of the Second World War. For three brutal years Judy suffered with her crew, surviving on scraps, living in the unforgiving harshness of the jungle and at the mercy of brutal Japanese guards. She befriended Frank Williams, a young British sailor who shared his rice rations with her.

The Prisoners of War were ordered to board *SS Van Warwyck*, where they would be transferred to Singapore. But the Japanese refused to allow Judy to follow her comrades. Her friends, though, refused to leave her and smuggled her on board the vessel in a sack. The following day, *SS Van Warwyck* was torpedoed by a British submarine who were unaware the ship was full of Allied POWs. Five hundred of the 700 crew died, but Judy was among the survivors. She was reunited with her friend Frank Williams at the next POW camp.

In 1945 Judy was sentenced to death, but escaped, only reappearing once her captors had gone. The camp was soon liberated.

With the war over, her friends helped smuggle her to Liverpool in England. In 1946 Judy received the Dickin Medal. Her citation read, 'For magnificent courage and endurance in Japanese prison camps, which helped maintain morale among fellow prisoners and also saving many lives through intelligence and watchfulness.'

She accompanied Frank Williams to Tanzania and died there in 1950. Judy's medal and dog collar are now on display in London's Imperial War Museum.

JUST NUISANCE

!!

Just Nuisance was a Great Dane from Cape Town, South Africa, and is remembered as the only dog to be officially enlisted into the Royal Navy. Nuisance served with the crew of *HMS Afrikander* from 1939 until 1944.

The dog was sold to Benjamin Chaney, who moved to Simon's Town to run the United Services Institute. The Great Dane became friendly with the locals and liked to sleep on the gangplank of docked ships. Being a 6ft long Great Dane, this earned him the nickname 'Nuisance' from the sailors trying to walk around him.

Nuisance enjoyed trains, and constantly travelled. His liberal use of the railways without paying his fares meant he was soon in trouble. Railway authorities contacted Chaney and warned him the dog would have to be put down if Nuisance didn't stop his anti-social behavior. Naval Command were having none of that. They officially enrolled Nuisance into the Royal Navy, meaning he now had free rail travel. He was given the forename of 'Just' and his official occupation was 'bone crusher'. Nuisance's religion was listed as 'Canine Divinity League (Anti-Vivisection)' and he was promoted to Able Seaman in recognition of his unofficial service prior to joining the Navy.

Just Nuisance never went to sea and took on only those jobs he wanted. He picked and chose, excelling at escorting drunk sailors back to their bases. Like many sailors, his career was not squeaky clean, he fought other dogs, went absent without leave, and refused to leave a pub at closing time His punishment, tongue-in-cheek, for sleeping on a Petty Officer's bed, was to have his bones removed for seven days!

A car accident in 1944 meant Nuisance was

discharged from the Navy. He died later that year, having been put down on the advice of a veterinary surgeon. Nuisance was buried with full military honours, even receiving a gun salute and the playing of the Last Post.

A statue in Jubilee Square of Nuisance continues to watch dutifully over the docks of Simon's Town to this day. Simon's Town holds an annual dog parade where a lookalike is selected and an exhibition in the town's museum ensures the memory of this beloved dog is never forgotten.

THE KATYN MASSACRE

!

The German invasion of western Poland on 1st September 1939 sparked World War Two. On the 17th of the same month, in collusion with the Germans, the Soviet Union invaded eastern Poland, after Stalin had successfully concluded negotiations to end hostilities with the Japanese. By mid-October Poland was crushed, and the Nazis and Soviets met in the middle, shaking hands and smiling for the cameras. Tens of thousands of Polish military were taken by the Red Army as prisoners of war, deep within the Soviet Union. This was war, there was nothing untoward about that.

In 1941, with Operation Barbarossa having now turned Germany and the Soviet Union into bitter enemies, the Polish government-in-exile operating from London decided to bury the hatchet with Stalin and agreed to help form a Polish army attached to the Red Army. This was where things got awkward.

Now that they were allies, Polish general Wladyslaw Anders asked for the release and return of 15,000 Polish officers to join the new army. Stalin hesitated. In December he finally responded, claiming that the Polish POWs had already been set free, but had wandered off into Manchuria (!) and that nothing had been heard from them since. Anders was disturbed by this account, but there was a war on, and he had no choice but to take the Soviets on their word.

If we take this as an isolated incident, this then becomes a mind-boggling case of Nazi Germany being, in some sense, the good guys. In 1942, as the eastern front raged, locals told the Axis forces about the site of a massacre committed by the Soviets. The Germans investigated and discovered thousands of Polish dead; soldiers, police officers and intelligentsia, all executed and piled on top of each other, many in Polish military uniforms – and the uniforms were fresh, they would have been killed very soon after being captured. The German investigation revealed that the slaughter took place in 1940. Stalin, with his usual flexibility of the truth, replied that the thousands of dead Poles were builders and workers who were in fact killed by the Germans. The Red Cross stepped in and their findings agreed with the German version of events.

For a man like Joseph Goebbels, this was music to his ears – there could be 12,000 dead. The discovery of the massacre was filmed, propaganda was pounded out, and international journalists descended. *Here* was a demonstration of the barbarism of Bolshevism, and proof of the threat to Western civilization posed by the Red Hordes. The hypocrisy and audacity of this propaganda coup is breathtaking in the light of the Nazis' brutality and appalling cruelty, all brought to the world's gaze a few years later.

The Polish government-in-exile were understandably outraged, and their own investigation into what happened was stonewalled by the Soviets, so on 25th April 1943 diplomatic relations ended. Stalin simply set up his own Polish government-in-exile made up of sycophants and yes-men.

This embarrassing incident was difficult for men like Churchill and Roosevelt. They had to balance honouring their commitment to their free Polish allies with keeping Stalin and the Red Army onside. The alternative was to risk turning the war into a three-way conflict. In the end, pragmatism won over idealism; and the Western leaders responses to the brutality of the Soviet Union became ever more uncomfortable and dismissive.

After the war a US inquiry found the Soviets responsible for the massacre. Once again Stalin stuck to his guns, and the Polish government, now a communist puppet-state deep behind the Iron Curtain, supported his version of events.

It was not until the 1990s that Russia revealed documents exposing the truth, that there were in fact up to 22,000 victims – even more than Goebbel's estimate. In 2010 the Russian government did the honourable thing and officially denounced the Katyn Massacre and put the blame at the door of Stalin and the Soviet Union.

Monuments to the massacre can be found in Britain, Russia, Ukraine, Canada, Austria, South Africa, the United States and, of course, the homeland of the inconvenient victims, Poland.

KISKA ISLAND

!!

The summer of 1943, a year and a half since the Japanese had woken a sleeping giant with their surprise attack on Pearl Harbor. The United States of America was on the warpath, and the war was going in their favour. However the Japanese still held two of their islands, Attu and Kiska, in the Aleutians off Alaska, which they had captured the previous year.

Under Operation Cottage, the US and their Canadian allies launched an amphibious attack on Kiska from opposite sides of the island. A pre-invasion bombardment peppered the island, warships fired off 330 tons of shells, the Eleventh Air Force dropping 424 tons of bombs.

34,426 soldiers landed and fought inland through the fog for two grueling days. 'Intense days of fighting followed', but this wasn't the Japanese defenders, it was the Americans and Canadians shooting at each other, mistaking each other for the enemy. By the end, the Allies suffered 313 casualties at the hands of the Japanese ghosts.

The Japanese had actually evacuated two or three weeks before the attack. The only inhabitants were a group of dogs, who had been left behind and greeted the troops when they landed.

KUGELPANZER

!!!

The Second World War was a time of great innovation and technological advancement. Some inventions were groundbreaking, others were dismal failures, and some were simply bizarre.

The Kugelpanzer (Ball Tank) is one of the mysteries of the war. Next to nothing is known about it. The most widely accepted theory is that it was a prototype created by the Germans and had been shipped to Japan, presumably as part of their dubious Axis alliance, when it was captured by the Soviets at Manchuria in 1945.

What was the purpose of this tank? It was shaped as a ball, with a track either side of an eye slit, which leads to the conclusion it was a prototype reconnaissance vehicle. Its armour was 5mm thick, and the strange vehicle was to be fitted with a machine gun - in Germany an MG34 or MG42, although in Japan it would have had a Type 96.

Similar ideas had already been conceived, particularly during the First World War, such as the One-Wheeled-War-Tank, the Treffas Wagen, the

Tumbleweed Tank and the Tsar Tank. Clearly there was an appetite for Ball-Tanks, but these have never come to a practical fruition.

The Kugelpanzer is still on display at Kubinka Tank Museum, Moscow Oblast, Russia and continues to intrigue experts and enthusiasts to this day.

KURT GERSTEIN

!

Kurt Gerstein's story is one of the enigmas of the war. He was either an SS war criminal, a heroic whistleblower, an inside man, a frightened liar – or some combination of them all.

Born to a Lutheran family in Munster, Germany in 1905; his mother died when he was young, and his father was a judge. He joined the Nazi party in 1933 and struggled to reconcile his religious faith with the movement. A performance of the play *Wittekind*, which attacked Christianity, offended Gerstein so much he spoke out and was beaten up for his troubles. He was arrested in September 1936 and imprisoned for five weeks when he was found in possession of anti-Nazi pamphlets which he had hoped to distribute. That led to his being expelled from the party. But thanks to his father the judge, who had friends in high places and who was able to pull some strings, Kurt was reinstated on 10th June 1939.

Around this point things get murky, and experts and investigators start to disagree. According to some sources, Gurstein found out his sister-in-law, Berta Ebeling, had died mysteriously in a psychiatric ward. Gurstein had heard rumours of the euthanasia program and joined the SS to go undercover and find out more. Other experts aren't convinced, stating that the chronology of his joining the SS and his sister-in-law vanishing cannot be verified, and she may in fact have been alive when he enlisted.

Now an undercover spy, or proud member of the SS, he was assigned to the Waffen-SS 'Hygiene Unit', where he contributed greatly to projects to provide safe drinking water and deal with vermin issues. With the coming of the Final Solution, the murder of all Jews, his role would change. He was soon involved. For example, one of his tasks was to ensure the efficient and timely delivery of Zyklon B to Auschwitz. He would later witness the horrors of the camps for himself.

He claimed he was appalled by what he saw and made efforts to inform foreign diplomats and religious leaders. According to him, he wanted to pass on the truth to the wider world, which was at the time ignorant of the scale of the murders. His appeals for help fell on deaf ears.

In April 1945, Gerstein surrendered himself to the French. He said he did this because he wanted the world to know what had really happened. His statements to the French authorities gave vital and accurate information about Belzec – but other evidence was problematic. He grossly over-exaggerated some claims, stating 25,000,000 had died, and claimed to witness events that didn't happen.

For reasons that remain uncertain, Gerstein hanged himself while in custody in July 1945. Perhaps he was overcome by grief at his failure to stop the Holocaust, and his inability to pass on his warnings to foreign powers; perhaps he was terrified of being tried as a war criminal; perhaps he was murdered - we can only conjecture. In August 1950, a denazification court found that Gurstein was indeed a war criminal – a subsequent campaign saw him pardoned in 1965.

So was Kurt Gerstein a war criminal? Was he a martyr going undercover to expose the death camps? Was he a man whose conscience had caught up with him, and who tried to jump ship in the last month of the war? It is likely we will never know the truth. The man remains a mystery, with supporters and detractors arguing their own opinions, but with little proof of what sort of individual he truly was.

THE LAMBETH WALK

!!

Viral hits don't belong solely to the age of YouTube and the Internet. *The Lambeth Walk* is one of the most memorable songs of the wartime era, from the 1937 West-End hit *Me and My Girl*. The song inspired its own dance craze, a strutting cockney jig made famous by the hilarious Lupino Lane.

The Lambeth Walk craze swept the nation, with even King George VI himself joining in with the famous 'Oi!' and it crossed the Atlantic. Britain's paranoid Mass Observation Unit, which reported on the morale of the country, even devoted a chapter of their 1939 book to it. The song was popular in Germany too, much to the lament of die-hard Nazis.

The Ministry of Information used it for their own ends. One of their number, Charles A. Ridley, mockingly edited Leni Riefenstahl's bombastic Nazi masterpiece, *The Triumph of the Will*, by humorously cutting the film. In his edit, *Lambeth Walk – Nazi Style*, the legions of soldiers are shown marching in time to the song. Their SS goose-steps fall perfectly in time with the music. The uncredited film was distributed to newsreel companies to do with as they pleased.

Joseph Goebbels, the Nazi Minister of Public Enlightenment and Propaganda saw Ridley's cut. It is reported he was so furious that he stormed out of the room, kicking chairs, shouting and swearing. As a result, Ridley earned a place on the *Sonderfahndungsliste G.B.* colloquially known as the Black Book, a list of people to be exterminated if Britain was conquered.

Perhaps the legacy of the song is perfectly summed up in *The Times* newspaper in 1938, 'While dictators rage and statesmen talk, all Europe dances — to The Lambeth Walk.' Take that, Gangnam Style!

THE LYKOV FAMILY

!!

It is said that ignorance is bliss, and for one Russian family, in a war that claimed more than 20,000,000 of their countrymen, this must arguably be the case.

In 1936, under threat from communists, a couple, Karp and Akulina Lykov, who were 'Old Believers', fled with their two children. Two more were born to them while in self-imposed exile. The family of six lived apart from society in the vast wilderness of Tashtypsky district of Khakassia, Siberia.

The troubles of the war passed them by. The family seems to have had no outside contact until 1978, when a geologist's helicopter accidentally came across their dwelling. When outsiders finally spoke to the Lykov family, they were not even aware that the Second World War had happened. When offered the chance to reintegrate into society, they declined.

All of the family were dead by 1988 except the fourth child Agafia Lykova, who had no human contact except her family for her first 35 years. She was born in 1943 and continued to live alone and self-sufficiently until 2016 when she was airlifted to hospital. Agafia did not like the modern world -- the unbearable noise and air quality of the cities made her feel sick and busy roads were terrifying. She happily returned to the wild once her hospital visit was over.

Perhaps Bear Grylls could learn a thing or two from her?

MADAGASCAR PLAN

!

The Nazis were clearly obsessed as to what to do with all the Jewish people throughout Europe getting on with their lives and generally minding their own business. The 'final solution' to this 'problem' is horrific and well known, but there were other plans long before that. One of the oddest was the idea of deporting Europe's Jewish families to the African island of Madagascar.

Mass deportations were seriously considered, and conversations between Germans, Poles, French and Britons took place to discuss it. Based on detailed reports from the French Foreign Office, the island of Madagascar, a French colonial possession seemed a suitable option. The plan being for a million Jewish people a year to be transferred to the island over a four-year period, though it was argued the island could not support so many.

Finance for this project was to be found from the confiscated income and property of the Jewish people themselves. The Reich were prepared to allow the Jewish citizens of Madagascar to have their own administration and government (in the areas not needed for military purposes), although the island would be under the command of a police governor of the SS. Also, the Nazis believed the concentration of so many people in one place and at the mercy of Nazi Germany would ensure the good behaviour of the USA and its Jewish population.

An intercepted letter from a top Nazi Franz Rademacher discussing the plan contained the following:

'Use can be made for propaganda purposes of the generosity shown by Germany in permitting cultural, economic, administrative and legal self-administration to the Jews; it can be emphasized at the same time that our German sense of responsibility towards the world forbids us to make the gift of a sovereign state to a race which has had no independent state for thousands of years: this would still require the test of history.'

After the *Luftwaffe* failed to defeat the RAF or force a surrender in the Battle of Britain, the Reich shelved this idea. On 10th February 1942, the plan was officially abandoned and the 'evacuation to the east' (Holocaust) was their insane proposal. The Nazis can't take full credit for this idea of mass deportation, though. The concept of deportation of Europe's Jews to Madagascar was originally conceived by German scholar Paul de Legarde in 1885. In 1937, the Polish investigated the proposal themselves, though they concluded the island could only support a few hundred families at most.

Despite Nazi plans to stop a Jewish homeland that would 'require the test of history', the state of Israel was created in 1948, just three years after the war ended.

THE MAGINOT LINE

!

The First World War had devastated France. Four years of brutal, near-static fighting achieved little, except millions dead and millions more wounded physically and psychologically. The Great War, allegedly in the name of liberty, had resulted in little more than bankrupt nations, crumbling empires and fascist and communist dictators springing up everywhere across a ruined continent.

With a bitter Germany growing increasingly vocal and militaristic, the French were taking no chances. In the 1930s the French began to construct a series of fortifications along their border with Germany. Named after the Minister of War, Andre Maginot, this impressive chain of forts, including twenty-two huge fortresses and thirty-six smaller ones, was believed to be impenetrable. Any German attack would surely be deterred and, if not, the line could comfortably hold off any attack long enough for reinforcements to arrive.

The Maginot Line is in this book not because there

is anything particularly weird about it - it was conceived and built with skill and imagination - but for the fact that it was a complete strategic failure. It led to a degree of confidence in French thinking, ignoring the competence of German military planning. After a year of the 'phoney war', when little happened in the West, the German *blitzkrieg* avoided the fortifications. Instead, the German forces bypassed them and advanced through Belgium. Since 1918, methods of waging war had changed with the advent of planes and tanks. The Maginot Line was a relic of the past. The British, French, Dutch and Belgians were caught on the back foot, and, with the exception of the British, all would be conquered. As for the British themselves, they were forced to scramble back to Britain via Dunkirk.

With the French armistice on 22nd June 1940, the invincible fortresses became redundant. The soldiers defending it, who were willing to fight on, were ordered to march out and surrender, spending the rest of the war as forced labour or in POW camps.

In 1944, roles were reversed, with the Germans defending the line against the Americans – who took a page from the German military planner's war book, and largely by-passed it.

THE MANNERHEIM RECORDING

!!

The Hitler and Mannerheim recording was the secret tape of a 1942 conversation between the German leader and Carl Gustaf Mannerheim, Finland's commander-in-chief.

It was the 4th June, and Mannerheim's 75th birthday, so Hitler decided to pop by and pass on his best wishes. Finland at the time was a co-belligerent of the Nazis, although this alliance was based pragmatically on the survival of his nation. The Soviet Union had made their intentions clear, and the last-minute withdrawal of Allied support in the 1939 Winter War left Finland stuck between a rock and a hard place. Better to fight one megalomaniac than two at the same time. Mannerheim was involved in a delicate game and was embarrassed to learn that Hitler was coming to see him. Mannerheim was keen not to give the Fuehrer's arrival the appearance of an official, state visit, so they met in secret aboard Mannerheim's train for dinner.

Thor Damen was an engineer for the Yle broadcasting company and was permitted to record the beginning of their conversation; the official birthday congratulations and Mannerheim's official response. Unknown to Hitler however, the recording carried on in secret for a further eleven minutes. Upon realising Damen was still taping, the furious SS demanded he stop immediately. He ended the tape, but bizarrely, rather than destroying it, the SS allowed him to keep it as long as he promised to seal it up and never use it. Damen handed over the tape to his employer Yle, who kept the tape secret until 1957, when it was publicly announced and made available.

The recording gives an interesting insight into Hitler's candid thoughts. He is clearly sincerely shocked by the production capability and fighting power of the Red Army and dismayed by the Italians crumbling in the face of the Allies. He also discusses Romanian oil fields.

It was one of only a few surviving recordings where Hitler is not hysterically shouting, and the only one in which he speaks candidly and casually. There is no doubt that Hitler's power was in his voice and the skilled rhetoric that he knew stirred up his people. Here, in the tapes, he was more natural, less careful as to what he allowed let slip. Away, as he thought, from recordings, he was less cautious about what the public might learn.

What is weird here is not the secret recording, but the interest it has generated. It says much about the morbid fascination we have for Hitler and the myth he tried to create for himself that to hear him speaking normally is a revelation. Many thought it must be a hoax. Even Hitler's bodyguard, when hearing the tape, was not entirely convinced.

The train coach where this meeting took place can be visited to this day. You'll find it plonked next to a Shell garage off a main road near Sastamala.

MASS-OBSERVATION

!!

The Mass-Observation project was a 1937 initiative set up by South African communist journalist, Charles Madge, and two of his English friends, Tom Harrisson and Humphrey Jennings. Their idea was to highlight the disparity between what the heavily censored newspapers were reporting and what people on the street actually thought. They published their manifesto for the concept as being *Anthropology at Home*.

Ordinary folk were asked a series of random (and frankly, quite odd) questions: about behaviour at war memorials, the behaviour and gestures of motorists towards each other, and people's behaviour in bathrooms. And they were asked to keep diaries of their thoughts and feelings on the 12th of each month. This led to negative reactions to the first report, published in 1937, since the opinions within included responses to the Coronation of King George VI and Queen Elizabeth after the Abdication that diverged from the intended propaganda. However, Mass-Observation was soon recognised as a valuable tool. In 1939, when Mass-Observation showed that the public was not responding well to a poster campaign, the Ministry of Information tweaked their propaganda accordingly.

Some people were (understandably) perplexed by the project, feeling it was an inappropriate and unnecessary intrusion into people's private lives and thoughts. Useful information included the average time to drink a pint -- about 7.3 minutes and that men drank fastest on a Friday, and slowest on a Tuesday. Another respondent moaned at the lack of charisma of Winston Churchill. 'He's no speaker, is he?' they complained.

'Liking' your partner was said to be the most important aspect of keeping a marriage going. The Lambeth Walk dance craze puzzled some participants, with one observer duly noting the men were holding the women inappropriately. Skippy, their pet rabbit went missing, wrote one, only to discover years later that Skippy had been served to them as dinner due to rationing. A father whose child was evacuated to the countryside, was upset by the 'fancy manners' his offspring had picked up.

After the war, a 1949 report from a gay man explains what a lovely time he had in Brighton, which even then was becoming a haven for homosexuals and those with alternative lifestyles. Others reported what a pain their neighbours were.

The interviews are a remarkable and charming glimpse into the past, and the sheer variety of the comments shared by the public is often amusing and poignant. For those of us in the modern age who are annoyed by the thousands of questionnaires, feedback forms and surveys that seem to appear out of nowhere, perhaps we can aim some of our grievances at Mass-Observation for starting them all.

The Mass-Observation archive can be accessed on the internet today. *Britain by Mass-Observation* (1939), published by Penguin, is another fascinating read.

MICKEY MOUSE

!!

With the war raging, and the imminent threat of biological and chemical weapons, gas masks became the must-have essential. Countries were seeking ways to allay the fears of their citizens, particularly children. After the 1940 attack on Pearl Harbor, America was taking no chances and distributed gas masks to its citizens, but it was important to prevent panic and keep the public's fear under control. One of the ways this was achieved was by using Mickey Mouse gas masks.

Walt Disney's Mickey Mouse was well known, first being introduced in 1928 in the famous *Steamboat Willie*. A thousand were made, the masks fitted with the smiling face of the comic mouse and were specially designed to fit those aged between 18 months and four years old, costing $1.25.

Thankfully, the need for gas masks never arose – perhaps the world was still horrified by the use of mustard gas in the First World War. Interestingly, even in his final desperate months, and tormented by his growing delusions, Hitler refused to entertain the use of biological weapons.

Few Mickey Mouse gas-masks have survived into the present day, and their creation, though understandable and well-meaning, has not aged well – looking to a modern eye like the stuff of horror movies and nightmares. That being said, the desire for some sense of normalcy, and for children to know the world had not gone completely mad, was important. Of Walt Disney's most memorable films, *Pinnochio, Fantasia, Dumbo* and *Bambi* were all released during the war years.

THE MIDWIFE OF AUSCHWITZ

!

S tanisława Leszczyńska was born to a devout Catholic family in Lodz, Poland in 1896. She spent her childhood in the Brazilian city of Rio de Janeiro, married in 1916 and returned to Poland – enrolling in the midwifery school and raising a family.

With World War Two marching on apace, Leszczyńska and her family did their bit to try to help the Jews of Lodz ghetto, smuggling in food and false papers. The local neighbourhood police caught her, and in an act of infamy, handed her to the Gestapo. Naturally, the entire family had to be punished. Two of her sons were shipped off to Mauthausen-Gusen, her husband and one son managed to escape capture, while Stanisława and her daughter Sylwia, a medical student, were taken to Auschwitz on 17th April 1943.

The Leszczyński women were assigned to the Auschwitz infirmary, where they became familiar with Dr. Josef Mengele. What happened to them and what they witnessed is the stuff of nightmares, but we shouldn't shy away from it. We owe it to them to know their stories.

Unbelievably, Auschwitz had a 'maternity ward' – which is odd enough. Pregnant women arriving at the site were normally sent straight to the gas chambers; if they didn't know they were pregnant until later – a bullet would do. So with this in mind, the existence of the ward seems bizarre.

The horrible reality of the place began to sink in for the Leszczyński women. The so-called nurses already there took no part in the births, their job was to immediately snatch the newborns from their mothers and drown them in buckets or barrels. When Stanislawa discovered what was expected of her, she refused.

Whilst the other 'nurses' went about their business, the new Leszczyński additions helped care for the mothers and, in the midst of squalid and appalling conditions, and without any equipment, gave it their best shot. With no option, they welcomed the little arrivals - although it was greeting them at the doorway to hell. Stanisława prayed for each and every tiny soul she delivered and baptized those who were Christian. She became affectionately known as 'the Mother'.

Her kindness cost her, she was physically, mentally and emotionally exhausted and the work was back-breaking. Her refusal to kill the babies constantly got her in trouble, even being scolded by Mengele. *What was the point of helping them? They were going to die as soon as they were born anyway. There was nothing to be done.* That may be, but *she* wasn't drowning babies in buckets: that was someone else's choice; that was on someone else's conscience. Surprisingly, despite her refusal to do Mengele's bidding, no punishment came, and Stanisława continued her work.

Some babies who were 'Aryan' enough were snatched from their mothers to be adopted as part of the SS' *Lebensborn* project and sent to new homes. Despairing mothers would often kill their young rather than let them fall into the hands of the enemy. Mysteriously, a handful were allowed to keep their babies, but why, and for how long, and what happened to them, is unknown.

The statistics are grim and upsetting, but we owe it to the victims not to ignore them. It is estimated of 3,000 babies born in Auschwitz, 1,500 were drowned, 1,000 died of cold or starvation and 500 were taken by the SS to be raised in Nazi Germany.

The work must have felt utterly, cruelly futile. If one, just one, newborn could survive being born in Auschwitz and escape hell with their mother, it would be miracle. But Stanisława was a realist: miracles didn't happen in Auschwitz. It was better to forget hope and carry on with the work.

Stanisława and her daughter survived the war, remaining at the camp until its liberation on 26th January 1945. She returned home and was reunited with her other children, though was heartbroken to discover her husband was dead, having fought and died in the Warsaw uprising. She continued her work as a midwife and only spoke of her ordeal when retiring in 1957. An account of her experiences, *The Report of a Midwife from Auschwitz*, is freely available. She passed on in 1974.

As for the maternity ward: it was not the case that one baby escaped with its mother… *thirty* did. Maria Saloman, one of those mothers would later say, 'To this day I do not know at what price [she delivered my baby]. My Liz owes her life to Stanisława Leszczyńska. I cannot think of her without tears coming to my eyes.'

Hospitals, organisations, a street in Lodz and a road in Auschwitz are all named in her honour. A campaign from admirers to have the midwife of Auschwitz canonized and declared a saint continues to this day.

THE MONKEYS OF GIBRALTAR

!!

The Mediterranean island of Gibraltar, off the coast of Spain has been part of the British Empire since the 1713 Treaty of Utrecht. During the war its strategic location, essentially controlling, as it did, the entrance to the Mediterranean Sea, made it a vital point for domination.

The civilian population were evacuated, and it became a target of bitter contention. Germany's Operation Felix, the invasion of Gibraltar, was stopped because Fascist dictator Francisco Franco, playing a delicate balancing act of neutrality, would not allow foreign troops to travel through Spain.

But was there another, more indirect way, by which the island could fall? Gibraltar is shared with a second population: Barbary macaque monkeys, the only wild monkeys of Europe. A legend states that as long as the monkeys live on the island, Britain's rule of it will never falter. In 1942, news reached Churchill that the monkey population was falling at an 'alarming rate'. Critically, only seven known macaques were known to have survived. Churchill went into action, ordering that reinforcements be brought in from the woodlands of Morocco and Algeria to replenish their strength.

The British Army cared for the monkeys. They even employed a guardian holding the post of 'Keeper of the Apes' (even though they were monkeys). Their job was to keep track of the animals, listing their dates of birth and controlling their diets. Births were announced in the local newspaper, *The Gibraltar Chronicle*.

Though the legend was safe, and the monkeys were brought back to strength, human/macaque relationships were not always friendly. In 1944, British troops executed Tony, the ape colony leader. Tony had become a nuisance and violent, entering people's homes and attacking other monkeys. He was succeeded by six-year-old Pat. Today, there are estimated to be 160 - 300 of the monkeys living on the island.

The sovereignty of Gibraltar has remained contentious, with Spain continuing to stake a claim. However, referendums conducted in 1967 and 2002 found that the population rejected leaving Britain.

MR. DOKTOR

!

Henryk Goldszmit, better remembered by his pen name Janusz Korczak, is one of the gentler heroes of the war. His kindness and compassion was an astonishing example of selflessness.

Born in 1878, he was a Polish Jew who in later life became a children's author and teacher, affectionately known by the children close to him as Pan Doktor (Mr. Doctor). He despised corporal punishment and all violence towards children and would go on to become director of the *Dom Sierot* Jewish orphanage in Warsaw.

In the aftermath of the German invasion of Poland, the orphanage was forced to relocate to the overcrowded and squalid ghetto in 1940. Despite opportunities to escape and save himself, Korczak chose to go with the children.

In August 1942, with the Nazi's 'final solution' in full force, the occupiers came to collect the 192 orphans. They were to be taken to Treblinka extermination camp, where they would be murdered.

The children couldn't be helped, but the Polish resistance offered to save Korczak. Once again, he would not abandon the children. He refused to be liberated and went with his charges to Treblinka.

The tragic scene of Korczak, his assistants, and the column of little ones leaving the orphanage must have been haunting. The children, from little tots to teenagers, were dressed in their best clothes, each with their favourite book or toy and holding hands with each other.

Once more Korczak had a third opportunity to save himself; it is alleged that an SS officer recognised the man as the author of his favourite children's book. The SS officer, depending on the source, either offered to help him escape, or to send him to Theresienstadt, where he at least had a chance of surviving. Once more Korczak said no, if his children were 'unworthy of life' and the powers-that-be determined they must be murdered; then he would die as one of them. With immeasurable inner strength and courage, he had made his choice.

And so the little column marched off, like some nightmarish distortion of the Pied Piper of Hamelin. Wladyslaw Szpilman, whose memoirs became the famous book *The Pianist*, gave a distressing report of what he saw that day:

'He told the orphans they were going out into the country, so they ought to be cheerful. At last they would be able to exchange the horrible suffocating city walls for meadows of flowers, streams where they could bathe, woods full of berries and mushrooms. He told them to wear their best clothes, and so they came out into the yard, two by two, nicely dressed and in a happy mood. The little column was led by an SS man.'

Korczak was with them at the end, Mr. Doktor did not leave his children for one moment. They were not left alone. As the metal door slammed shut, and the poison gas choked them, they all went to the meadows of flowers together.

Two of Korczak's children's books have been translated in English, *King Matt the First* in 1986 and *Kaytek the Wizard* in 2012. Statues of Janusz Korczak and his children can be found in Warsaw and Jerusalem.

NAZI CHIC

!!

There is a sub-culture in East Asia which, if not massively offensive to Westerners, is at least very peculiar. Cosplay, when participants dress up in costumes to imitate film heroes or characters from books, is popular in the West, however, in East Asia a minority of youngsters dress up as SS and Nazi officers.

Examples of this 'Nazi chic' include, in 2016, a Taiwanese school holding a mock Nazi parade, students saluting each other with 'sieg heils' and carrying Swastika flags. Elsewhere, there have been Nazi themed bars, such as the *Soldaten Kaffee* in Bandung, Indonesia, which was finally shut down in 2017 after protests. Even the most forbearing were appalled by *Jail* in Taipei, Taiwan – a concentration camp themed restaurant, complete with toilets labeled as 'gas chambers', a mural of pathetic inmates behind barbed wire, and photographs of actual historical atrocities on the wall. A small fried chicken takeaway, called *Hitler*, was threatened with a lawsuit by KFC for copying the image design of Colonel Sanders for the dictator.

Sony Music apologized for Japanese girl band Keyakizaka46 dressing up in outfits similar to the SS. South Korean pop group Pritz apologized too for a similar gaffe, as did Indonesian pop star Ahmad Dhani.

The occasional foible happens in the West too. In 1999, James Brown, the editor of men's magazine *GQ* was fired when Field Marshall Erwin Rommel was listed as one of the best dressed men of the 20th century.

One expert, Elliot Brennan, of the Institute for Security and Development Policy, investigated this phenomenon. He stated that it is difficult for Asian peoples to relate to the Western view of Nazism. Hitler and the European war happened far away, and the same taboos do not exist for them. This is more due to ignorance than anything malevolent. It was a demonstration, in much the same way that rebellious Western teenagers would wear Che Guevera or Mao ZeDong clothing, or display Soviet paraphernalia in an attempt to shock their elders and those of a conservative disposition. The same cannot be done in Asia, as these symbols are in fact the symbols of 'the man' – meaning that, oddly, Nazi chic is considered an anti-establishment equivalent.

Perhaps Nazi chic can best be summarized as simple ignorance of the historical underpinnings. In the same way that we in the West may be ignorant of the taboos of the Asian war, in which higher estimates propose that as many as 20 million Chinese were slaughtered by the Japanese, something which sullies diplomatic relations to this day. Likewise, Asians are less aware of the impact of the Nazi atrocities in Europe.

Things are, however, moving in the right direction. Most reasonable people would agree that the right to shock and offend, express themselves and show individuality is important. On the other hand, mutualism, respect and sensitivity to each other is equally important. If we can avoid the banal hysteria that threatens to derail and debase both sides of the argument; education and healthy dialogue will surely only help these contrasting views reconcile sooner rather than later.

THE NIIHAU INCIDENT

!!!

The Niihau incident is one of those rare events that somehow doesn't quite ring true, it feels more like a boy's own comic adventure, but it did happen and the facts speak for themselves.

It was the 7th December 1941 and Shigenori Nishikaichi, a Japanese pilot of a Mitsubishi Zero fighter had just taken part in the Pearl Harbor attacks. Returning from the bombing run, Nishikaichi's squadron was attacked by American Curtiss P-36A fighters. The Zeroes made quick work of these and won the dog fight, but the pilot's plane had been hit, his engine was failing, and he fell behind his comrades.

During the pilots' briefing that morning, the men had been told that, if any of their aircraft were damaged, they should attempt to land on the uninhabited island of Niihau, the westernmost island of Hawaii, and await rescue. Nishikaichi found the island and began to descend. As he did, he discovered something wasn't right -- he saw buildings. Braced for a rough landing, he came down, hit a wire fence and crashed.

Niihau was in fact inhabited. It was owned by the Robinson family, who bought it from King Kamehameha V in 1864. The island was off limits to outsiders, and only the native Hawaiians and a handful of others lived there; the Robinson's themselves living on the larger island of Kauai.

A local, Howard Kaleohano, came across the wreck and the dazed and confused pilot. He took his papers and sidearm, and then helped Nishikaichi. The pilot was even fed breakfast. Blissfully unaware of the attack on Pearl Harbor, they were curious as to what a Japanese pilot was doing so far from home.

Japanese-born Ishimatsu Shintani also lived on the island as a beekeeper. He was asked to translate. Shintani, who only wanted a quiet life, begrudgingly accepted. Upon speaking to the pilot, it is said that he turned pale and walked off in disgust.

There were two other Japanese on the island who could help, Yoshio and Irene Harada, and it was their turn to speak to Nishikaichi. The pilot informed the Haradas of the attack on Pearl Harbor, and that Japan and the United States were now at war. The Haradas didn't pass this on.

Oblivious to the day's attack, the Hawaiians had a party for their guest, complete with guitar songs – but the party was about to turn sour. The island had a battery operated radio, and this radio announced the attack. The Haradas had a hard choice: loyalty to Japan, or loyalty to America. The locals couldn't tell the Robinsons on Kauai, what was to be done?

Nishikaichi confided in the three Japanese locals. Whatever was said, soon Shintani went to ask

Kaleohano for the pilot's papers to be returned, but Kaleohano refused. Events soon spiralled out of control. Sources diverge slightly, but the main events are clear.

It appears Yoshio Harada stole a shotgun and attacked Kaleohano's house to get the papers back by force. Kaleohano managed to escape and hid the papers at his mother-in-law's. Despite an emergency naval ban that had come into effect, Kaleohano and five others rowed to Kauai to warn them of the two-man invasion. Meanwhile Nishikaichi and Harada had taken one of the machine guns from the crashed plane and were shooting into the air, demanding the return of the papers.

Eventually the Japanese took a married couple, Benehakaka 'Ben' Kanahele and Kealoha 'Ella' Kanahele captive. However the captors were weak and tired. Ben and Ella pounced on them. In the ensuing fight, Harada shot Ben three times, but Ben had enough strength to throw the pilot through the air, his wife smashed the pilot's head in with a rock and Ben slit his throat. Harada, seeing this, turned the gun on himself and pulled the trigger.

Next morning, by the time Howard Kaleohano, the five Hawaiians, Robinson and the army authorities arrived, the invasion was over. Shintani was interned, finally receiving citizenship in 1960. Irene Harada was jailed until 1944. Ben Kanahele recovered from his wounds and received the Medal of Merit and the Purple Heart, his wife received nothing. Nishikaichi's Zero is on display to this day at Pacific Aviation Museum Pearl Harbor.

The fact that the Haradas, who previously had been considered to be good neighbours, could have changed their allegiance so quickly shocked the US authorities. This incident must have contributed to Executive Order 9066, where some 120,000 Japanese-Americans were taken from the West Coast and interred for the remainder of the war.

NIMROD

!

E dward Elgar was a British composer, famous
for his *Pomp and Circumstance Marches*. To this
day, *Land of Hope and Glory* is belted out
annually by a packed hall during the prestigious last
night of the Proms musical event.

He is equally remembered for his *Enigma Variations*,
composed of fourteen variations of an original theme.
Variation 9, called *Nimrod*, is now inextricably linked
with the war in Britain; always played at
remembrance services, and is synonymous with the
Cenotaph memorial service on Remembrance
Sunday. Hazy memories claim that this music was
played at Winston Churchill's funeral and, although it
would certainly have been fitting, in fact it was not.
Churchill's funeral was codenamed Operation Hope
Not, something which would have fitted his sense of
humour to a tee.

Elgar enjoyed cryptology and would often write to
his friends in riddles and puzzles, probably to their
occasional chagrin. His greatest puzzle, which has
never been solved, is the mystery behind the *Enigma*

Variations itself. This piece, written between 1898-1899, has intrigued music lovers ever since. The puzzle first came to public attention during the programme notes from its first performance. It was tantalizingly noted:

> 'The Enigma I will not explain – its "dark saying" must be left unguessed, and I warn you that the connexion between the Variations and the Theme is often of the slightest texture; further, through and over the whole set another and larger theme "goes", but is not played... So the principal Theme never appears, even as in some late dramas – e.g. Maeterlinck's *L'Intruse* and *Les sept Princesses* – the chief character is never on the stage.'

So what was the mystery behind the Enigma? It has certainly captivated musicologists, historians and armchair detectives ever since. The proposed solutions are as varied as they are countless, and there are far too many to list. They range from hints at the overlaying theme, musical notes translating to letters in the alphabet, secret codes or identifying a hidden overarching theme. Some of the suggestions are so mind-bogglingly complex, they themselves would take teams of professionals to unravel. Simpler answers include playing *Twinkle, Twinkle, Little Star* over the piece in minor key, or Martin Luther's *A Mighty Fortress,* though a Catholic composer using a protestant anthem seems unlikely. Bob Padgett, perhaps the world's most fervent Enigma codebreaker, has taken on this unlocking of this riddle – even turning to Christianity, the bible and God for an answer.

Elgar vaguely teased a solution a few times but not agreeing with any of the answers put forward to him — he took his secret to the grave in 1934. So what was it? It's unlikely we will ever know. Perhaps it was something so infuriatingly simple as to pass us all by, or so convoluted as to be indecipherable by anyone.

Elgar's work, particularly *Nimrod*, received an astonishing new lease of life when it was used as the inspiration for the soundtrack of Christopher Nolan's powerful 2017 film *Dunkirk*. The composer Hans Zimmer was touched by *Nimrod*, and his own equally moving version, *Variation 15*, plays out as the story ends.

Thanks in part to *Dunkirk* and its fifteenth variation, Elgar's *Nimrod* is back with a vengeance. Peculiarly, this majestic piece of music has found a solid home in advertising, it's appeared everywhere from commercials for beer, banks, pastries, cars, shops, dog food and even Marmite!

OPERATION CLAYMORE

!

Operation Claymore, named after the Scottish sword, was a daring raid on the Norwegian Lofoten Islands. On 4th March 1941 British commandos, supported by other units, were ordered to destroy a number of important factories used by the Reich. The mission was a success: eleven (or eighteen) factories, five ships and 20,000 tons of shipping were destroyed. In addition, around 800,000 gallons of oil went up in smoke and hundreds of Germans were taken prisoner.

The raid was so unexpected that many locals assumed it was a training exercise. Not a single Allied soldier died in the raid: only one received a mild injury (an accidental, self-inflicted wound). Fortunately the defenders were caught unawares, and 228 soldiers surrendered with little resistance, though this lack of action was disappointing to many of the more gung-ho commandos.

With the humour typical of the British at the time, one officer sent a telegram from the local post office to an *A Hitler*, 'Herr Hitler. Reference your last speech:

you said whenever British troops land on the continent of Europe, Germany will face them. Well, where are they?' Some commandos made a day of it, even taking a bus ride to a local seaplane base!

Three hundred and fourteen Norwegians volunteered to join the Allies as part of the Free Norwegian Forces and returned with the commandos to Britain. Some British officials did not see the strategic value in commando raids such as this, but they incensed Hitler, who became convinced Britain was going to launch a full scale attack on Norway. This led to him taking men from theatres elsewhere to defend the long Norwegian coast. Crucially, the commandos also came across codebooks and parts of an Enigma machine, which could be carefully studied at Bletchley Park and helped Alan Turing and his team understand the workings of the complex Enigma machines.

Winston Churchill passed on his personal thanks, 'To all concerned, my congratulations on the very satisfactory operation.'

PAVLOV'S HOUSE

!

The Battle of Stalingrad was the bloodiest battle in human history. Added to the ideological importance of a city named after the Soviet leader - the showdown here was violent and unforgiving, either the Soviet defence would crumble or the Axis forces would perish. Neither dictator would consider backing down, and there were no other options. Stalin's order No. 227 stated 'not one step back'.

Germany, Italy, Hungary and Romania lost the equivalent of 100 divisions between them. 'It is hell.' said one soldier, 'No, this is ten times worse than hell.' he was corrected.

Nothing encapsulates this battle better than 'Pavlov's House', named after Sergeant Yakov Pavlov. The house was strategically important. It overlooked the Volga embankment and gave a clear line of sight in three directions. Layers of barbed-wire were installed and mines laid, machine guns were placed in every available window, doors were barricaded – the defenders were planning for a long fight, and they were not disappointed. Ongoing fighting and the sounds of war made sleep almost non-existent. It's even claimed that the piles of German dead were so high, the Soviets were forced to sneak out to knock down the walls of corpses.

The fighting from July 1942 was savage: bitter house-to-house fighting, with men constantly in danger among the ruined buildings. Each scuffle was a fight to the death.

Remarkably, the Soviets held out, despite constant attacks, for two months. On 25th November 1942, Pavlov and his men were finally relieved by reinforcements. They became national heroes.

The Battle for Stalingrad raged on for months, officially ending on 2nd February 1943, at the cost of over a million lives. Stalingrad was the first time Hitler openly admitted he had suffered a defeat.

The Soviets joked that the fight for Pavlov's house was costlier to the Germans than the entire invasion of Paris.

The last survivor of Pavlov's defenders, Kamoljon Turgunov, died on 16th March 2015. The remains of the bricks of the house have been used to build a memorial.

THE PEOPLE'S COURT

!!

The *Volksgerichtshof* ('People's Court') was created by Hitler in 1934. The legal system of Germany, even under his rule, didn't suit him. He was infuriated that all but one of the defendants at the Reichstag fire trial of 1933 were acquitted. The People's Court is listed here because it was so farcical, that it made even the most corrupt show trials and kangaroo courts look legitimate in comparison.

The president of the People's Court was Roland Friesler, a particularly cruel and sadistic man. Under his dominion the farcical courts lost any semblance of justice and legal procedure. Friesler was a master of surreal theatrics that turned the courtrooms into pantomimes. Here oratorical skills and a cunning tongue were more important than facts and context. Defendants were sent to their deaths, sometimes on less than two pages of text. The death sentence was liberally imposed on 'antisocial parasites'. Being defeatist or being found to be involved in a 'work slowdown' could also send you to the gallows. Brother and sister Sophie and Hans Scholl of the White Rose movement, an anti-Nazi academic leaflet campaign, were beheaded by guillotine.

The defendants' lawyers, were, of course, part of the system. Their roles seem to have been reduced to little more than explaining the process (whatever that means in regard's to the People's Court). Sophie Scholl's defence lawyer even lambasted his client, telling her she would pay for her crimes! The defendants would then be hauled in front of the judge, who generally insulted them, while the defence lawyers remained silent. A person could be in and out, and sentenced to death, in fifteen minutes.

The most famous trial was that of the conspirators of the 20 July plot to assassinate Hitler. Friesler talked over any attempts made by the defendants to speak. He called Colonel-General Erich Hoepner a 'schweinhund'. To Field Marshal Erwin von Witzleban, who was given oversized clothing and denied a belt to hold them up, he shrieked, 'You dirty old man, why do you keep fiddling with your trousers?'. The shambolic farce of this 'courtroom' must have left all who were thrown in front of it with a depressing realisation of their fate. Attempts to take part were pointless and would only have appeared to legitimize the trial. Most must have simply wanted it over and done with as quickly as possible. In all, Friesler decreed 5,000 death sentences in his three year period.

Many of the 20 July plotters met a grisly end, being hanged by rope so thin it was known as piano wire. Various estimates suggest it took between 45 seconds to 10 hours (!) to die. This was all filmed and sent to

Hitler for his viewing pleasure. Many, such as the stoic Admiral Wilhelm Canaris of the *Abwehr*, were given the added humiliation of being naked when they were executed.

A surviving movie reel shows one of Friesler's trials. As a defendant explains his motives, and his disgust at Nazi murders, the judge bellows like a demented villain, reminiscent of Oliver Twist's Mr. Bumble: 'Murder?' he shouts, 'You miserable scum!'

There are many different theories as to the end of the People's Court. It was either bombed by the USAAF 8th Air Force on 3rd February 1945 – crushing Friesler under a collapsed pillar, while he was still holding his files; or he made it out onto the street before bleeding to death on the pavement; or it was bombed by the British – killing Friesler but sparing two women in the dock. Either way, one lucky escape, was the 20 July conspirator Fabian von Schlabrendorff. His trial was meant to be held later that day, but the bombing of the courtroom destroyed his file. He survived the war and lived on to 1980. When Friesler's body was brought to the hospital, it is claimed that a worker said 'It is God's verdict.' Friesler was buried ignominiously with an anonymous gravestone in his wife's family plot in the Waldfriedhof Dahlem cemetery.

Apart from the Chief Prosecutor, Ernst Lauz, who was imprisoned for four years, no one was punished for involvement in the People's Court. The perverse excuse for this was that, under the laws of the Reich, their actions were completely legal. Yet so too were the gas chamber killings of the SS concentration camp guards, the murders of the Einsatzgruppen, and the other despicable acts of elements of the regime. Those people were punished for their atrocious crimes. But the 570 judges and prosecutors involved in the People's Court went free, and they would continue in the lucrative world of the law for the remainder of their cosy careers.

THE PHANTOM FORTRESS

!!

It was 23rd November 1944, when an Allied airfield in Belgium had an unexpected visitor. A solitary B-17, one of the bombers nicknamed a 'Flying Fortress' for their toughness and weight of armaments, was heading their way a bit too fast for the liking of the ground crew. It must be an emergency landing. Not that there was anything odd about that, it happened all the time.

The B-17 came in on a wing and a prayer, it was a clumsy landing, but it landed in one piece. The ground crew waited for the pilot and crew to disembark, but for twenty minutes it just sat there with the propellers whirring and the engine running. Eventually, the observers decided to investigate.

The plane, unbelievably, was empty. Like a flying version of the Mary Celeste, the ghost ship that haunted sailors nightmares, there was simply no one on board. The plane had all the signs of life, including half-eaten chocolate bars, the log book's cryptic final entry simply read 'bad flak'.

An investigation by the 8th Air Force revealed that the plane had taken part in a bombing run of German oil refineries. The crew were tracked down elsewhere and were all alive and well.

It turned out that during the run, the B-17 was hit by enemy fire, an engine was damaged and the bomb bay was hit, although miraculously it didn't detonate the payload. The plane was damaged, an engine was down, and with fears that the bombs could go off any moment, the crew made the justified decision to parachute out. The last crewman putting the plane into autopilot before he jumped out. The pilot Harold R. DeBolt would say, 'I'll be damned if I know why the bombs didn't explode'.

What happened next is murky and hotly debated, but it seems that with the perfect combination of the right speed, the failed engine making the plane lose altitude and a huge pinch of luck the plane appeared to those on the ground to be making a half-decent landing.

Many accounts of pilotless planes flying on were accounted for during the war, though this is the only known successful landing. There is a lot to this account that raises the eyebrows of historians. Nevertheless, the phantom fortress and its spooky landing still intrigues servicemen, military buffs and paranormal enthusiasts alike!

THE PHOTOGRAPH ALBUMS OF AUSCHWITZ

!!

'The Auschwitz Album' is a one-of-a-kind collection of photographs taken from inside the infamous concentration camp. The album contains 193 images, evidencing the horror of Auschwitz-Birkenau.

The upsetting images storyboard the nightmarish experience of a newly arrived group of Hungarian Jews in 1944. We follow the victims through their journey, from the unloading of the trains and the 'selection' process of those who were deemed unfit for work being sent to their immediate deaths, where they have to seemingly wait their turn on the grass outside a crematoria. An area mockingly named as *Kanada*, (Canada) 'the land of plenty', where the stolen belongings of the victims were sorted is also pictured.

The evidence seems to suggest the photographs were overtly taken by the SS themselves, but if this is the case – why? The Nazis were careful to keep the death camps a secret from the outside world and it is

156

unclear what official purpose the images would serve.

The Auschwitz Album is not in this book because it is weird in itself, or even that the motives or identities of the photographer(s) have never been revealed. It is here because of its astonishing survival through the decades, particularly when we consider the zealousness of the SS in destroying all evidence of their crimes.

Even more remarkable than its survival, is the unbelievable way it was discovered. A survivor of Auschwitz, Lilly Zelmanovic, was recovering in the now liberated Dora concentration camp after the liberation of the Allies and was resting in an old SS barracks. In the barracks, she happened to come across the album in a nearby cupboard, not only containing pictures of herself and her family but many of her neighbours. This is even more surprising when you consider that Dora is over 400 miles away from Auschwitz!

Other than a handful of surreptitious and blurry photographs taken by brave sonderkommandos, this album is the only photographic evidence we have of the inner workings of Auschwitz. The contents of the album were later used in war-crime trials. Lilly Zelmanovic donated the album, minus pictures she donated to friends and other survivors earlier, to Yad Vashem in 1980 and it was published later that year. Despite speculation, the identity and motive of the original photographer(s) will likely never be certain.

Contrasted with the wholesale slaughter of the *Auschwitz* Album is the *Höcker Album*, named after Obersturmfuhrer Karl Höcker, who is assumed to have been its original owner. The 116 pictures in this album, without context, seem harmless enough, but knowing that the smiling faces within belong to the wardens of Auschwitz make it all the more sinister.

Höcker and his colleagues, along with the Helferinnen (women helpers) are pictured joking and laughing, enjoying a getaway to the lakeside resort of Solahutte, 30 kilometres from the main camp. An accordion player leads a sing-along with 70 SS men. Höcker sits among the Helferinnen enjoying blueberries and sunbathing in deck chairs. All this in late 1944, a particularly busy and brutal time for the death camp, the crematoria at some points being unable to keep up with the queue of new corpses.

The Hocker album is unique and priceless, identifying key architects of the Holocaust. Particularly important were the images containing Dr. Josef Mengele, the eight pictures of him within are the only photographic evidence we have that he served at Auschwitz.

This album was found in circumstances equally as extraordinary as those of the Auschwitz Album. An American intelligence officer was billeted to a Frankfurt apartment after the war. Within this apartment, he casually happened across the photo book. He donated it to the United States Holocaust Memorial Museum in 2007, under the condition his identity would be kept confidential.

Höcker was put on trial in Frankfurt in 1965 and sentenced to seven years in prison. He was released after five. He was sentenced to a further four years imprisonment in 1989 and died in 2000, aged 88.

PINK POWER

!

The unusual story of pink spitfires led some to believe it must be a hoax, or the result of too many pink gins. Why on earth would the RAF paint their most prized aircraft in such a garish colour?

And yet the RAF did use pink spitfires, and they were surprisingly effective.

In simple terms, the colour theory for traditional spitfires was that when seen from above, their mottled camouflage greens and browns would blend in with the ground below, and when seen from below, their pale blue/grey undersides would blend in with the sky. At the time of sunrise and sunset however, pink is an excellent choice. The colour was used by the RAF's photographic reconnaissance unit, whose pilots would fly behind enemy lines and photograph targets.

It wasn't just spitfires that were pink, ships appeared to disappear on the horizon when painted a similar cover, giving the Royal Navy a natural advantage. First used in World War I, the colour became known as Mountbatten Pink after Lord

Mountbatten, and was used by several warships, despite protestations from more traditional sailors. Experts disagree on how successful the grey-mauve colour actually was.

THE PINK TRIANGLES

!

Homosexuals were one of the myriad groups persecuted by the Nazis in Germany. By 1945, 100,000 had been arrested, 50,000 were in prison, and up to 15,000 were in concentration camps – the pink triangle on their clothes marking out their 'crime' for all to see. This figure of course doesn't include homosexuals who had found themselves in trouble for other reasons such as being social democrats, Jews or 'asocials'.

The treatment of gay men was appalling. In the curious homo-erotic world of Nazism, they were considered the lowest of the low. Many within the Nazi ranks were homosexual, or had homosexual tendencies, but those who were 'hard' could hide it, those who were 'soft' (read effeminate) weren't so lucky. Homosexuality and sexual promiscuity were commonly used for ad hominem attacks on the opponents of the Nazis, designed to wreck their reputations and social standing, even when utterly without foundation.

Homosexuals could sometimes 'redeem'

themselves with acts of manliness or accepting 'cures'. These 'cures' included taking hormone supplements and undergoing experiments on their testicles. Gay men would often be forced to perform sex acts on female inmates, lesbians would have to do the same with men in camp brothels. The cruel dog-eat-dog world of concentration camps saw them abused and attacked by fellow inmates.

Unlike other categories of prisoners, who could look forward to freedom and liberation with the arrival of the Allies, homosexuals had no such guarantee. Depressingly, many of them found they were left in, or sent back to, prison to complete their sentences, because homosexuality was a crime in the eyes of the liberators as well. One instance showed the West German government had kept survivors on a sex offenders' list long after the war.

Gay people received some respite in the 1970s when 'sodomy laws' were repealed. The German government apologized in 2002. Testimony of these 'forgotten victims' who died before the world was ready to accept them is, as a result, tragically sparse.

PRIVATE SNAFU

!!

rivate Snafu was a bungling cartoon character who served in the United States army. His name comes from a slang acronym used by the armed forces to describe the general chaos and make-it-up-as-you-go-along attitude of war. To more respectable audiences S.N.A.F.U was bowdlerised as 'Situation Normal, All *Fouled* Up'.

Private Snafu served in cartoons from 1943 to 1945 and was voiced by Mel Blanc, the legendary voice over actor who also gave us Bugs Bunny, Daffy Duck, Porky Pig, Speedy Gonzales and countless others. The cartoons were written by a team including Theodor Geisel, better known by his pen-name Dr. Seuss.

Not all soldiers serving in the armed forces were literate. Many received inadequate education. Private Snafu was on hand to help, his light-hearted cartoons show him demonstrating how to behave. Therefore, by getting things wrong, the audience could understand the need for military protocol and correct behaviour.

The cartoons were intended solely for a military audience, and a whole range of paranoid security measures were put in place to keep Private Snafu a secret from the enemy and civilians. Workers on the animation were only given ten celluloids at a time, to stop them working out in advance the plot of the cartoon!

Private Snafu may not have made it into this book if it wasn't for his episode 'Going Home'. In this 1944 cartoon, Snafu is returning to the United States on leave. While home he wanders around town, carelessly blabbing military secrets to civilians. In the next scene he is in a cinema with a young lady, and this is where things get interesting.

In the cartoon clip, the cinema screen shows a secret weapon that is being developed by the Americans. This 'bazooka bomb' has, at a push, some similarities to the atom bomb, which in the real world was being developed as part of the top-secret Manhattan Project. The bomb then obliterates a Japanese island to which the narrator jokes, 'What hit you, Tojo? Wouldn't you like to know.'

It's been alleged that this cartoon disturbed the powers that be so much they had the cartoon pulled and it was never shown. This seems somewhat over the top, given Private Snafu's track record it is unlikely he had prophesied nuclear warfare. What *is* unusual though is it is not clear exactly why this particular episode was never released and there are several theories on this.

Could the cartoon have been a bit too close for comfort to the top-secret atomic bomb? Given the behavior and paranoia of all governments across the world at the time it is not outside the realms of possibility.

Snafu finally revealed himself to the civilian world in a 1999 VHS collection. He is now in the public domain and his cartoons can be viewed freely on the internet.

PROPER PROPAGANDA

!!

Propaganda during the Second World War was an unavoidable aspect of daily life. It must be a situation that is hard to relate to for those of us in the West born too late or too young to remember the war or the decades afterwards. The idea that you must always be alert to the ominous drone of the air-raid sirens as you went about your business, or that your home could be destroyed in an aerial bombardment at any moment is very hard to comprehend. But those who lived through the war knew it was perfectly possible that the Wehrmacht could soon be marching through the streets, with all the chaos, fear, death and destruction that that would imply.

Against this backdrop we can understand why propaganda was so vital to all sides of the conflict. For those interested in the psychology of the past, propaganda posters are a great glimpse into the (understandable) paranoia, hysteria and concerns of those who created them, and the message they thought it was necessary to promote to everyone else.

All of these posters served some sort of purpose, and modern cynicism means it is often hard not to scoff at some of them, because to us they are now often unintentionally humorous or offensive. Those in government at the time knew that war had evolved. The Great War had changed much, and this latest conflict with Germany would create a huge strain, both in terms of morale and in the nation's resources, and it was vital to have and maintain full support for the war at home.

While propaganda was nothing new, it came into its own during the Second World War. British posters were, in the main, created by the controversial Ministry of Information, a government department that was dissolved soon after the war and probably one of George Orwell's inspirations for 'Big Brother'. Many contemporary members of parliament were very disturbed by the agenda of this department and protested that there was a very real danger that Britain could ironically sleep-walk into becoming the fascist, brain-washed state with which they were at war.

The messages behind most of these posters is overt and obvious. The well-known, but never actually distributed, 'Keep Calm and Carry On' posters are still recognisable to us today, over 70 years later. Other messages may verge on the bizarre to those who never knew the horrors of the conflict first-hand. One poster shows a soldier and his partner on a sofa with the message 'Keep mum (stay silent), she might not be so dumb', implying that his girlfriend may, at best, be a loudmouth who will report his military operations to everyone in town and, at worst, be a

Gestapo agent who had been planted into his home. This isn't to mock the sentiment, but simply to point out how difficult it is for a modern mind to understand.

Other posters urging mothers to evacuate their children away from towns as refugees to find safety in the countryside, or even abroad to the security of Canada or other parts of the empire are quite shocking. Still more so are those which implied that people taking a day off work due to sickness could be shirking, or that those who lost a tool at work were aiding Hitler, are quite unsettling even now.

American propaganda was often racist, showing rat-like Japanese. One dramatic poster, featuring two creepy children in their gas masks and proclaiming 'Dear God, keep them safe!' is still striking.

On the Axis side, they were oddly obsessed with reminding Allied soldiers, particularly Americans, that their women were back at home, probably sleeping with someone else and that 'the negroes' were now running the country.

Soviet sources claim they recovered Nazi prototypes for German TV shows which would be played on huge screens in public areas. Overseen by engineer Walter Brutsch, show ideas allegedly included 'Family Chronicles: An Evening with Hans and Gelli', a reality TV type show, where Hans and Gelli would demonstrate the Aryan ideals of home life. Executions would also be filmed and shown to the public.

RECON FLIGHT 300

!!!

December 1942, and the war was reaching its zenith. No one could confidently predict how it would all pan out: who would win, who would be crushed. The Allies were growing in strength, but Germany and Japan were still enormously powerful and dangerous. It was now that the war presented one of its most chilling, and still unexplained, mysteries.

Three hundred miles north of Bergen, Norway, the RAF reconnaissance flight 300 was taking photographs of key locations deep within the Scandinavian country. Upon returning to Britain and having the film developed, shocked analysts caught a glimpse of something unnatural. When they magnified the shot, something … appeared. The aircrew had inadvertently taken a picture, and provided real evidence of, a Norwegian mountain troll.

Or so the story goes.

There is no need to look deeply into this. It is plainly a hoax. The actual photograph could be from the time, but it is clearly doctored. The picture, which was probably altered with Photoshop or a similar digital editor, shows what appears to be the outline of a gigantic troll moving through the fog, towering over a forest below.

This prank is worth noting, though, because it is so modern and demonstrates perfectly the nonsense (before, during and after events) that serious academics, historians (and writer-researchers!) often find themselves having to sift through to find the elusive nuggets of truth. The 'culprit' behind this jape is unknown - the evidence appears to point in the direction of a talented freelance illustrator, photo-manipulator and artist.

Even if we consider this story and photograph with a completely open mind and give them the benefit of the doubt, there are so many questions that the whole matter quickly becomes laughable. For example: who and what was 'Recon Flight 300', and what was their actual military objective? Why, in other words, were they overflying and photographing a section of forest? If they *didn't* see the troll, why take a picture of the woods? If they *did* see the troll, why didn't they at least report it, and take many more pictures to verify their sighting? Finally, how could such a gigantic creature feed, eat, shelter and breed – while its Norwegian neighbours remained blissfully unaware of its gargantuan presence?

My own personal opinion, though not corroborated in any way, is that this picture was a tie-in to generate buzz for the mockumentary film

Trollhunter, directed by André Øvredal and released in 2010.

RESCUE DOGS

!

For those of us who have never experienced it, we can only imagine the claustrophobic nightmare of being the victim of a bombing raid, trapped under piles of brick and dust, choking, perhaps being slowly crushed, in the dark, with limbs injured, and in a great deal of pain. This was the fate of untold civilians throughout the war who were victims of the Blitz and similar air attacks.

Imagine then, being met by a wet nose and a pair of furry paws. For 100 lucky victims of the London Blitz, this was Rip the dog. Rip himself had been a victim, being found as a stray after a 1940 attack on Poplar. He happened across an air raid warden, E. King, King threw the dog some scraps in the hope the dog would go away, but he didn't, and an unlikely friendship was formed.

Rip was a natural for search and rescue operations and helped those scrabbling through the rubble for survivors. He was said to be unbothered by dangers such as fire and smoke and the horrible drone of the air raid sirens. What is so remarkable about Rip, is unlike later dogs, he had no training and did his work on his own volition. The success of Rip gave the authorities thought for the use of dogs in future search and rescue operations.

Rip was awarded the Dickin Medal and wore it the rest of his life. In 2009, the medal was auctioned and sold for £24,250.

There were countless other canine heroes, and recipients of the Dickin Medal, such as Jet the German Shepherd from Liverpool who saved around 150 people. Jet would howl every night, but he finally stopped at the same time as the air raid attacks ceased.

Crumstone Irma worked with her owner, Margaret Griffin, and another dog, Psyche, both Irma and Psyche were German Shepherds. Irma was able to give different sounding barks depending on whether those under the ruins were dead or alive.

Two young girls had been trapped under a building for two days, Irma barked 'alive!' – she wouldn't give up. The rescuers around her thought, 'Poor Irma, she must have got it wrong. No one's coming out of that ruin alive.' But she got it right. To the amazement of the rescue workers, the girls were pulled out and survived.

Thorn, another German Shepherd, once detected the scent of a family trapped under a burning house – how a dog could pick up the scent among the smoke and flames baffled the rescue workers – but Thorn was right, and another family was rescued.

It is interesting to note that 'Alsatian' and 'German Shepherd' are terms for the same breed. The name was changed during the First World War. Fearing that people who kept a 'German' shepherd would be displaying an unwholesome affinity with the Hun enemy, it was decided to refer to the breed as Alsatian, after the Alsace region of France. The Americans changed the name to 'Shepherd Dog' in 1917. In the United Kingdom, the Kennel Club returned the breed to German Shepherd once more in 1977 - but 'Alsatian' continues to linger on as the colloquial name for the breed to the present day.

ROBINSON CRUSOE

!

The Warsaw Uprising was a brave action in August 1944 by the Polish to throw the Germans out of the city that they had occupied for five long and cruel years. The uprising was planned to coincide with the Red Army advance, and the Polish resistance fighters hoped to aid the Soviet attack to join in the liberation of their city, but the Soviet advance halted. It is suspected that Stalin had decided to leave the Polish, his former enemy, to their fate.

Unsurprisingly, without outside help, the German military overcame the resistance and destroyed over a quarter of the buildings in the city, in some areas going from house to house with flamethrowers. Including the buildings destroyed beforehand, Warsaw saw some 85% of all its buildings demolished during the war.

The Polish fought bravely, holding out for 63 days, but with little support, they could do no more.

There were some groups of survivors from the

uprising, and remarkably there were still Jews among them. Some took their chances and ran, while others decided their best hope was to stay and hide in the ruins until it was all over. Surely the Soviets would be there any day.

These survivors became known as the Robinson Crusoes of Warsaw, named after the eponymous hero from the famous 1719 book by Daniel Defoe, which followed the life of a castaway on a desert island who survived many adventures before finally returning to civilization. One survivor of Warsaw, David Fogelman, wrote 'We lived like Robinson Crusoes, with the one difference he was free.' Fogelman's fate is unknown.

The number of different groups of Crusoes, ranging from individuals to dozens, is believed to be as high as two thousand. Most were eventually caught and killed, and the stories of the survivors alone are known to us. That some groups survived so long is astonishing.

Warsaw was the bare husk of a city. Himmler had decreed 'the city must completely disappear from the face of the earth'. The Crusoes endured in maddening isolation, hiding like rats and scavenging, if strong enough, by night. Water was precious, and a good day was had by finding a toilet cistern or an old boiler. Finding a few scraps of food made for an excellent day. Survival was not easy. Many were finished off by the cold, as lighting a fire involved the risk of exposing their position to the enemy. The undying myth of drinking your own urine also took many lives.

There are many notable cases of Crusoes. One, or perhaps a collective, called himself Ares, after the Greek god of war and became a local legend. He would ambush enemy soldiers and graffiti his name among the ruins as a warning. On one victim he left a note, 'Ares is a ghost, not matter – your search for him is useless.' One story states Ares was dying of poisoning, after eating food that had been deliberately contaminated and left as a trap, not before firing off a few shots with his pistol into the enemy ranks and taking his own life. Another legend states that Ares arranged dead combatants sat in a circle and listening to a gramophone. When the enemy went to investigate, he ambushed them with grenades.

The most famous Crusoe was Wladyslaw Spilzman. He wrote his harrowing story in 1946, in a book called *The Pianist*, which was adapted to become

Roman Polanski's 2002 film of the same name. He was spared, and aided, by the chivalrous German captain Wilm Hosenfeld – who was made Righteous Among the Nations by Israel's Yad Vashem. Five years after the war Spilzman learned of Hosenfeld's identity and tried to help him, but he without success. The captain died two years later in a Soviet POW camp.

The Soviets – who had previously invaded Poland with the Nazis - left the Polish to it for three agonizing months. Even refusing permission for the planes of the Western Allies carrying aid to land. The Polish government-in-exile implored the Allies to assist, but they would not move without Stalin's agreement. Churchill asked Roosevelt and Stalin to take part, but they didn't. He eventually authorized clandestine RAF supply drops by night from Italian airfields, 223 sorties were made, but it was simply too little to be of much assistance. The Germans eventually abandoned the city in 1945.

THE SAUSAGE WAR

!

Before the war, Stalin and Hitler carved up Eastern Europe between them in secret talks. In these discussions, Stalin was given Finland – which he wanted back after they broke away from Russia following the Russian civil war.

Despite a ten-year non-aggression pact signed in 1932, on 30th November 1939 the Soviets bombed Helsinki, and the Winter War began. The British and French were outraged, and the Soviets were expelled from the League of Nations. But Britain and France had to tread carefully. They were already at war with Nazi Germany and taking on the Soviet Union too would have been suicidal. Most assumed Finland would crumble after a few weeks. There was nothing to be done to save the Finns from the Soviet onslaught.

Despite being overwhelmingly outnumbered, the Finns put up a brave fight, their knowledge of the land and the harsh winter of 1939 caused chaos for the Red Army. The Finns were like ghosts, suddenly appearing, fighting with determination and skill and then melting away into the snow after each fight – but one alleged battle was not quite so mysterious and romantic.

On December 10th it is claimed the Soviets launched a surprise attack on the Finns near the village of Illomantsi. The Finns weren't prepared and fled. But the battle took an unusual turn. The Finnish cooks had just finished preparing a batch of delicious sausages in their cooking tents, and the smell was too much for the attackers. The starving Russians stopped and began tucking in to the sausages. The pause gave the Finns long enough to regroup, reform, and counter-attack. Their ferocity and the unpreparedness of the Russian soldiers meant that only a few of the Soviets survived. It is claimed that many of the Red Army died with sausages still in their hands and their mouths. This incident would become known as 'the sausage war'.

Is the sausage war true? We have only the word of the victorious Finns, but it was not a surprising event. Throughout history, starving soldiers have been known to set aside their weapons when finding food and drink. It has been reported that Ludendorff's swift advance in 1918 was halted not by Allied counter-attacks, but by the discovery by German soldiers of stockpiles of food and wine. Exhausted and starving, the soldiers fell on the supplies and the German attack was halted. Still, the Sausage War does show the disorganization of the Soviet army, mostly caused by Stalin's paranoid purges of his military elite at the time.

The Finns held out long enough to force the

Soviets to reach a cease-fire. Later, the Finns were caught between a rock and a hard place. Finally, they felt forced to ally themselves with Nazi Germany, from motives of self-survival against the threat once more from Russia, though they did not join the Axis.

In the west the Allies understood Finland's unique position. The British formally declared war – probably to assuage Stalin – but America didn't bother. It is thought that the Finns' courage had an even more world-changing consequence: the poor performance of the Soviets was noted in Germany. Perhaps it stirred stronger ambitions in Hitler: perhaps the effectiveness of the Finns in the Winter War convinced him that an attack on Russia could succeed. Perhaps his eye turned, earlier than he originally planned, to the east.

The Soviet Union continued to deny the existence of the Molotov-Ribbentrop Pact long after the war, dismissing it as Western propaganda, until finally doing the honourable thing in 1989.

SONDERKOMMANDO ELBE

!

The beginning of the war demonstrated to the world the seemingly invulnerability of the Luftwaffe. No country on the continent had survived the onslaught of the German Blitzkrieg. Hermann Goering was so confident of his air arm that he left the destruction of the trapped pocket of men at Dunkirk to his airmen. Then they were to be entrusted with bringing Churchill to heel during the Battle of Britain. With the British gone, a jubilant Hitler boasted they would never return to the continent.

The war in 1945 was a completely different story. The Allies had air supremacy, and in some areas the Luftwaffe had ceased to exist. Sonderkommando Elbe was a last desperate gamble. Simply put, it was a unit designed to collide with enemy aircraft and knock them out of the sky. The plan was that the attackers would eject just as they were about to crash into their target, using their propellers like a circular saw. The optimal targets were the vulnerable points, the cockpit, the empennage and an area near the fuel system.

The stripped down planes only flew one mission on 7th April 1945. Their attack was arguably effective, with eight of fifteen Allied bombers being destroyed. However, it was never going to make a difference, and squandered those pilots and planes the crumbling Reich had left. Unlike the fanatical kamikaze 'divine wind' pilots of Imperial Japan, it was hoped, albeit unlikely, that the German pilots would try to survive their missions.

SOVIET APE-MEN

!!!

The tale of Ilya Ivanovich Ivanov, a Russian biologist and his 'ape-men' is one that should be approached carefully, and without getting swept up in rumour.

Briefly, the allegations go as follows: Ivanov gave a presentation to the World Congress of Biologists where he explained to his colleagues the possibility of creating ape-human hybrids. He'd had success with other animals, so believed this was a scientific possibility.

He went on with his experiments, setting off and travelling to the far reaches of the world. In the 1920s his trials involving the use of human sperm to inseminate female chimpanzees failed to produce any results. He then tried using ape sperm with human volunteers, though this failed when his Orangutan died on the way to Russia.

In the bewildering world of Soviet intrigue, Ivanov was arrested and exiled to Alma Ata where he would die in 1932.

In later years, tabloid newspapers got their hands

on this story, where they claimed Joseph Stalin had ordered Ivanov 'the Red Frankenstein' to create a mutant army of ape-men, who would follow orders without question and conquer the world! It's unlikely Ivanov would have ever been on Stalin's radar, and there is no evidence that either of them had the slightest interest in creating ape soldiers.

Some years after the war a creature called Oliver (1957 – 2012) was believed by some to be a human-chimpanzee hybrid. Science has shown this is clearly not the case and he's an ordinary ape but once again the myth never quite died.

SAVITRI DEVI

!!

Maximiani Portas was a French-Greek-Italian mystic who went by the pseudonym Savitri Devi. She is considered by some to be the founder of 'esoteric Hitlerism', the belief in the divinity of the Fuehrer.

After the First World War, Devi believed that Greece and Germany had been humiliated and unjustly punished as whipping boys for the bloody aftermath of the conflict, despising the harshness of the Treaty of Versailles. She blamed Judeo-Christianity for eradicating any memory of a heroic Aryan past, and believed, like many others at the time, that the Aryans descended from India.

Travelling to India, the sight of a white woman travelling fourth class by train raised the eyebrows of many and the British began to keep her under surveillance. She learned Indian languages, married a Brahmin, and went to work on her writings of a mystical Aryan utopia. Devi was an ardent admirer of Hitler, believing him to be an Avatar – an incarnation of the Hindu god Vishnu – as stated in her book *The*

Lightning and the Sun. She travelled the country giving lectures and quoting liberally from *Mein Kampf*. During the war, she even spied for the Axis, and passed on vital information to the Japanese forces.

In 1948, three years after the war, Savitri Devi travelled to Germany and began distributing leaflets boasting 'One day we shall rise and triumph again! Hope and wait! Heil Hitler!' This message was divinely inspired, she would write. Arrested and charged, she was sentenced to two years in prison, where she befriended Nazi and SS inmates, including a 'beautiful-looking' female warden from Belsen. After eight months she was released and deported. She then went on a 'pilgrimage' of Nazi sites. Rumours spread that Francoise Dior, niece of Christian Dior the fashion designer was her lesbian lover. She befriended the unrepentant Nazi, Hans-Ulrich Rudel, and wrote *The Lightning and the Sun* at his home.

Her later years saw her return to India with a collection of cats – and a cobra. She did not have the same disdain for animals that she exhibited towards humans. She travelled to England in 1982, dying the same year. Her ashes were laid to rest with full honours next to George Lincoln Rockwell, head of the American Nazi Party in Arlington, Virginia – now the site of a coffee shop.

What is weird here is how an animal-loving French-Greek-Italian mystic, the wife of a Hindu Brahmin, who befriended a swathe of neo-Nazis, could reconcile Hindu mythology with National Socialism, and how her occultist theories and cosmic inventions would be taken so seriously by some of her readers.

SEALAND V REGINA

!

The history of the Principality of Sealand is one of the most fascinating and charming curiosities of the modern age. It is a contender for the smallest country on Earth, has its own royal family, is not recognized by anyone internationally, and it encompasses solely one small metal and concrete platform just off Felixstowe, with no permanent population except a handful of security guards.

As part of Britain's defences during the Second World War, a chain of sea forts fitted with anti-aircraft guns were built in the North Sea to protect the country's vulnerable eastern flank. However, several of these forts were constructed in international waters and were outside British territorial waters and therefore jurisdiction, not that it would have mattered during the crisis and urgent need of war. Churchill would not have been concerned so long as Britain had her defences.

One of these sea forts called 'Knock John', abandoned at the war's end, lay invitingly in the

North Sea. The charismatic Major Roy Bates of the British Army sensed an opportunity that was too good to be missed. Major Bates travelled to the sea-fort and set up a pirate radio station. The British government weren't impressed and took legal action. Bates took on the might of the Crown in a legal battle, which he naturally had no chance of winning. The courts declared Knock John was within British territory. But why let the Crown pick the battlefield? Another fort, 'Roughs Tower', was seven nautical miles out and, in the eyes of their own law, beyond their three-mile grasp.

In September 1967 the Bates family, supported by a small contingent of friends and well-wishers, took over Roughs Tower, declared their independence and claimed sovereignty with the birth of the Principality of Sealand. His wife became Princess Joan.

The British establishment was infuriated. Some tried to claim, somewhat melodramatically, that they feared Sealand could be a 'Cuba off the east coast of England.' They blew up all the remaining sea forts and used helicopters to intimidate the Sealanders by hovering close above their platform. A demolition crew was to be sent to threaten the nascent nation with imminent destruction. Prince Michael, the son of Roy, fired off a few warning shots, the queen's men fled and the first battle of Sealand was a glorious victory. As British citizens, the police charged the Bates' men with fire-arms offences, the prosecution desperately trawling through 17th century laws to find an actual crime for which they could be convicted. Yet the judge agreed with the Bates – Sealand lay outside the rule of British law, and the English court had no authority in international waters. The case was thrown out.

Prince Roy had won. By 1975 Sealand had its own flag, constitution, national anthem, currency and passports. The rest of Sealand's colourful history is astonishing, there have been military coups and armed takeovers, diplomatic standoffs and there was even a government-in-exile!

Thanks to an overreach of British coastal WW2 defences, Britain has a nuisance neighbour which survives to this day. The current reigning monarch of Sealand is Prince Michael, son of Major Roy Bates. Prince Michael's 2015 book *Principality of Sealand: Holding the Fort* gives a fascinating account of the adventures of the Bates family. Prince Michael has three children himself, and the Royal line is well and truly secure.

I myself (RD) was so charmed by the story of Sealand that I have since become ennobled. My new title is Lord of Sealand (available from their official website with a certificate). The cash-for-honours fiasco, which shamed Britain, could be coming my way!

THE SEVEN DWARFS OF AUSCHWITZ

!

The Ovitz family, were entertainers known as the Lilliput Troupe. The Hungarian family included seven dwarfs who, because they were Jewish, eventually ended up on 19th May 1944 at Auschwitz. They are not in this book because there is anything remotely weird about them, but for the extraordinary way in which they were treated, and how they survived against the odds. An SS officer, noticing them disembark from their train barked orders to 'wake the Doctor', referring to Josef Mengele, known as the Angel of Death. The family waited nervously amidst the chaos of the train station as the rest of the crowd was moved on around them.

It was well known among his men that 'peculiar' people, such as twins, and hermaphrodites obsessed Mengele and the seven dwarfs were of equal fascination. The youngest of the family, Perla, asked a Jewish Sonderkommando where they were, and where the streams of people were going. 'This is no bakery – this is Auschwitz and you'll end up in the ovens too' he candidly replied.

The family intrigued Mengele, and they did not have to go through the process of shaving their heads and losing their clothes that the other victims did. Though receiving slightly more humane conditions, the dwarfs and their siblings were subjected to endless tests and cruel torture. If the females weren't wearing a full face of makeup, Mengele would notice and comment on this. Offset with Mengele's insincere charm was his power over life and death and the horrific way he would treat people with whom he had grown bored.

The Lilliput Troupe were performers, playing music and singing songs across Romania, Hungary and Czechoslovakia. They were forced to 'perform' at Auschwitz too, by standing on a stage naked, in front of an SS crowd, being prodded and leered over as specimens. Some of the things the family experienced and witnessed were so disturbing, they are perhaps inappropriate to mention in detail in a book like this. Some of these events were filmed, though the film reels are not believed to have survived.

They endured long enough to be liberated by the Red Army on 27th January 1945. They returned home to find it had been looted and, with nothing left to stay for, they moved several times before settling in Israel.

The last surviving dwarf Perla died in 2001 at the age of 80. Of Mengele she said 'If the judges had asked me if he should be hanged, I'd have told them to let him go. I was saved by the grace of the devil — God will give Mengele his due.'

Mengele, who spent his remaining years on the run in fear of discovery, fleeing across South America, was discovered drowned in 1979. To this day, Mengele's bones are at the Sao Paulo Institute for Forensic Medicine, occasionally being hauled out for medical students to study.

The 2014 book *Giants: The Dwarfs of Auschwitz* by Yehuda Koren and Eilat Negev explains their astonishing story further.

THE SHRUNKEN HEADS OF BUCHENWALD

!!

The long list of horrors that came to light after the war across Nazi-occupied Europe shocked the world. Since then, the crimes committed have lost little power to appall those who were born long after the atrocities. Some of them were so savage, pointless and inhuman, that it is tempting to believe that they are mere fictions, and never happened. Take, for example, two shrunken heads, alongside human skin, taken from the SS-Pathology department at Buchenwald concentration camp.

The testimony of Kurt Sitte, a Czechoslovakian doctor of Physics who had been a political prisoner in Buchenwald from 1939, sheds some light on this. Sitte revealed that the two heads belonged to prisoners who had escaped but were recaptured. They were subsequently beheaded on the orders of SS Doctor Mueller.

Some asserted that the heads were souvenirs or curios from South America, but science doesn't agree.

There is no evidence to support this claim.

One of the heads was produced as evidence by Thomas Dodd at the Nuremberg trials. The sheer barbaric lunacy of it almost made Dodd apologise for presenting it as an exhibit, but explained he felt compelled to let the court see it for themselves.

The shrunken head shocked the court. Many simply couldn't, or wouldn't, believe it was real. Evidentially it served little purpose, other than to demonstrate the kind of experiments conducted by Mueller and others. There it was, a hideous trophy displayed for all to see. A civilized Western nation, a Christian state, had experimented and shrunk a man's head. It was worthy of the most lurid fiction, or a gruesome Boy's Own adventure.

Francois de Menthon, the chief French prosecutor at the trials said, 'the work of twenty centuries of civilization, which believed itself eternal, [could be] destroyed by the return of ancient barbarism in a new guise.'

Buchenwald was unique in that it didn't carry the (false) motto of other camps, *Arbeit macht frei* ('work sets you free' – it didn't). Buchenwald instead went for *Jedem das seine* 'to each his own', a quote from Martin Luther. This sign, oddly, faced inwards for those inside the camp to see. It can also be translated as 'everyone gets what they deserve'. Perhaps those words came to mind for those who ended up in the dock at the subsequent war crime trials.

SILBERVOGEL

!

S ilbervogel (silver bird) was one of the proposals put forward for Hitler's ambitious Amerika Bomber project, with which he hoped to attack the US mainland. There was no real chance, even in 1942, of the Kriegsmarine ever being able to supply and protect aircraft carriers near enough the United States to pose any substantial threat to the US mainland. So could a bomber travel the 5800km journey itself?

Behind the complex concept was an equally complex design, formulated by Eugene Sanger and Irene Brant. The idea was, in simple terms, that the Silbervogel would be launched like a rocket from Europe and ascend to the fringes of space. Once there, it would travel across the Atlantic in a series of sub-orbital 'hops', before dropping its payload and returning home.

The Luftwaffe were impressed – but it was horribly impractical and expensive, and the limited resources of Nazi boffins were needed elsewhere.

After the war, with President Truman and Premier

Stalin at loggerheads, the Soviets tried to persuade Eugene Sanger, who was now living in France, into working for them. When their charm offensive failed, it is alleged they tried to kidnap him, which fortunately failed.

The United States were also impressed, and though the Silbervogel was a failure in its time and place, it is believed by some that the theories involved would go on to inform the scientists working on the NASA space shuttle design.

SIWASH

!

Siwash, from New Zealand, was a duck that served with the First Battalion of the Tenth Marine Regiment in the Pacific theatre. The legend says Sergeant Frank Fagin, a US marine, won the duck in a raffle (or a poker tournament) in 1943. Siwash would become the unofficial mascot of 2nd Marine Division. The duck also enjoyed beer, as long as it was warm, which appealed to the troops.

When the marines went into battle at Tarawa in 1943, Siwash valiantly fought alongside them. Earning a citation:

'For courageous action and wounds received on Tarawa, in the Gilbert Islands, November 1943. With utter disregard for his own personal safety, Siwash, upon reaching the beach, without hesitation engaged the enemy in fierce combat, namely, one rooster of Japanese ancestry, and though wounded on the head by repeated pecks, he soon routed the opposition. He refused medical aid until all wounded members of his section had been taken care of.'

Siwash, now a sergeant, also saw action at the battles of Saipan and Tinian. After the war, Siwash, according to the source, either took on the role of a Marine recruiter for the Korean War or retired at Lincoln Park Zoo in Chicago. Siwash died of liver problems in 1954.

But Siwash had managed to keep one secret from, but a select few, of its comrades during the entire war, *he* was actually a *she*, Siwash was a girl, one of only a very few cases - or perhaps the only one - of a recruit successfully hiding their gender to fight on the front!

SMOKY THE DOG

!!

Smoky the dog entered the war in mysterious circumstances. The Yorkshire Terrier was discovered by an American patrol in March 1944 in New Guinea, hiding in a foxhole. She was sold to Cpl. Bill Wynne for two Australian pounds, and backpacked with him through the unforgiving jungle. The dog did not appear to understand English or Japanese, so her reasons for being at the front are unclear.

Smoky survived 150 air raids and Wynne believe she saved his life by warning him of incoming artillery strikes, ducking in time to dodge a barrage that killed eight of his comrades.

During the bombardment of the Lingayen Gulf airfield on Luzon, her heroics came into their own. She aided the troops by running a telegraph wire for the Signal Corps through a 70ft long pipe. It is believed her courageous run saved 250 men what would have been the equivalent of a dangerous three-day task. It was Smoky's finest hour.

Smoky's positive impact on hospitalized soldiers

was noted, and the idea of therapy dogs was catching on. By 1947, 700 dogs were working in hospitals. Cute pictures of Smoky sitting in a GI's helmet and proudly standing over a trophy still survive.

Smoky became a national hero and after the war continued to entertain America by performing tricks such as riding a scooter, spelling her name and tight-rope walking. She performed 42 times on television.

Smoky died peacefully in her sleep in 1957 at the age of 14. A bronze statue erected in 2005 at Cleveland, Ohio, celebrates her remarkable life.

THE SPANDAU SEVEN

!

After the war and the subsequent Nuremberg trials, many of the Nazi leadership were executed for war crimes. A group of seven were instead jailed at Spandau prison in West Berlin. The group, known as the Spandau Seven, were Baldur von Schirach, Hitler Youth leader; Erich Raeder, Grand Admiral; Konstantin von Neurath, diplomat; Karl Dönitz, Admiral; Albert Speer, minister for war production; Walther Funk, minister for economic affairs and the enigmatic Rudolf Hess, former deputy of the Reich.

It was a complicated arrangement. The Americans, British, French and Soviets would each run the prison for three months of the year before handing over to the next. The prison was well guarded, with at least sixty soldiers, because it was feared that any remnants of the Nazi cause, if they existed, could try to rescue their leaders. The daily routine for the seven was strict and orderly, and communication with the outside world was, officially, forbidden. The 600 common criminals of Spandau were moved out of the 134 cells they shared to make way for the VIPs.

The Spandau Seven are not in this book because there was anything weird here - other than the idea of a prison run for just seven men – but for the childlike, petty rivalries that these former heads of the Reich indulged in.

Admirals Raeder and Dönitz made one team, although Raeder still had a private grudge from 1943 when Dönitz replaced him as head of the navy. Speer was an outcast, shunned by the others for disloyalty and his brown-nosing of the Allies. Hess was a loner, who cared as little for the other six as they cared for him. Shirach and Funk became best friends, and the social butterfly Nuerath fluttered effortlessly between the factions.

Speer kept himself busy, secretly writing two books and going on walking holidays in his imagination, using the prison garden for measurement. Raeder placed himself as head of the library, with Dönitz his assistant, and thus was 1943 avenged.

The most mysterious of the inmates was Rudolf Hess. His time in Spandau is as obscure as the reasons for his bizarre one-man flight to Scotland on 10th May 1941. Hess has given historians headaches ever since. He kept to himself, and even in the petty world of Spandau politics he wasn't popular. Constantly fearful of being poisoned, he was often bed-ridden, complaining of agony, real or faked, which saw him avoid having to work.

By 1966 all of the prisoners had been released except Rudolf Hess who, bizarrely, had the entire prison to himself for a further twenty-one years, until his death in 1987. The 93 year old apparently hanged himself with an extension cord in a summer house. However, the circumstances surrounding Hess's death are contentious. According to the British, attempts to let him go free were blocked by the Soviets. Hess's son believes the British murdered him in order to prevent him revealing embarrassing wartime secrets. Other historians state his suicide note was actually written in the 60s. Why Hess was the only one of the seven to actually serve a whole life sentence remains an intriguing question.

The prison was demolished in 1987 following Hess' death to stop it becoming a neo-Nazi shrine. A car park and shopping centre were built in its place. The Berlin Wall would come down four years later. The pop band *Spandau Ballet* take their name from the prison: 'ballet' being a grim reference to the frantic death throes of those hanged at the gallows.

STALIN THE POET

!

Ioseb Besarionis dze Jughashvili, later known as Stalin (Man of Steel), had a rise to power that was, in its way, as peculiar as Adolf Hitler's own. Both came from poor backgrounds, both had unhappy childhoods, both despised their fathers, had run-ins with the establishment, were no strangers to prison cells and shared unquenchable ambitions.

There is a further similarity in their creative streaks: Hitler was an artist and a poet, and Stalin himself was a poet before rising through the ranks during the Bolshevik Revolution, the events of which in 1917 turned Russia on its head and terrified the capitalists and imperialists of Western Europe.

Stalin became a fan of writers such as Goethe, Shakespeare and Walt Whitman. He wrote anonymously, using the pseudonym Soselo, and later attempts by his admirers to collate his works for publication were personally stopped.

How Stalin and Hitler could reconcile the kindness and beauty found within their prose with their actual actions cannot be easily understood. Stalin's poem

The Moon goes;

> Sail on, as tirelessly as ever,
> Above an earth obscured by clouds,
> And with your shining glow of silver
> Dispel the fog that now abounds.

> With languor, bend your lovely neck,
> Lean down to earth with tender smile.
> Sing lullabies to Mount Kazbek,
> Whose glaciers reach for you on high.

> But know for certain, he who had
> Once been oppressed and cast below,
> Can scale the heights of Mount Mtatsminda,
> Exalted by undying hope.

> Shine on, up in the darkened sky,
> Frolic and play with pallid rays,
> And, as before, with even light,
> Illuminate my fatherland.

> I'll bare my breast to you, extend
> My arm in joyous greeting, too.
> My spirit trembling, once again
> I'll glimpse before me the bright moon.

A second darker, more ominous poem goes as follows;

> He knocked on strangers' doors,
> Going from house to house,

With an old oaken *panduri*
And that simple song of his.

But in his song, his song
Pure as the sun's own gleam
Resounded a truth profound,
Resounded a lofty dream.

Hearts that had turned to stone
Were made to beat once more;
In many, he'd rouse a mind
That slumbered in deepest murk.

But instead of the laurels he'd earned,
The people of his land
Fed the outcast poison,
Placing a cup in his hand.

They told him: 'Damned one, you must Drink
it, drain the cup dry…
Your song is foreign to us,
We prefer to live in a lie!'

Like Hitler, Stalin never returned to his poetry once
he assumed power.

SWASTIKA NIGHT

!!!

The Second World War is *the* hotbed for alternative and speculative fiction, the likes of which the world has never seen before. No period of human history has fascinated writers and readers quite so much. And the most tantalising question is, 'What if the Nazis had won the war?' Famous examples include Robert Harris' 1992 novel *Fatherland* and the 1964 movie *It Happened Here*. This obsession continues to the modern day, with popular retellings such as the televised series *Man In The High Castle*, originally a 1962 novel by science fiction writer Philip K. Dick, and the BBC series *SS GB*, originally published in 1978 by Len Deighton.

There are so many hypothetical questions that intrigue us; what if Germany continued its relationship with China and did not ally with Japan; what if Japan attacked the Soviet Union instead of the US; what if Finland fell to the Soviet Union and the Molotov-Ribbentrop Pact was fulfilled; what if the US entered the war before Operation Barbarossa had commenced; what if Spain or Turkey joined the Axis;

what if Roosevelt did not stand or win a third term as US President, the list goes on and on.

Of the countless works to have been penned regarding this most famous 'what if?', surely Katharine Burdekin's *Swastika Night* must win the prize for the most imaginative. The book is not mentioned here because it is weird, but because it was written *before* the war. The grimly prescient book was first published in 1937, two years before the outbreak of the conflict.

The story follows an alternative history, one in which Germany and Japan have conquered the world. Set 700 years in the future, the story follows the protagonist, Alfred, an Englishman, who goes on a pilgrimage of holy Nazi sites, including a Munich plane that Hitler flew to Moscow to win the war. Hitler is remembered by the world as a seven-foot, blue-eyed, blonde deity. Women are reduced to the caste of baby-makers, shaven-headed pathetic creatures hidden from the world and used solely for breeding. As the story develops, and Alfred learns the truth behind the lies and horrors of the Empire, he believes a spiritual rebellion must happen urgently, and fears any armed conflict – which the Germans would win – would reassert the world's delusional belief that violence and strength of arms is linked to righteousness and the favour of the gods. At the end, soldiers beat Alfred so viciously that he dies of his wounds. In dying, he fantasises about finishing his book and exposing Hitler to show what sort of a man he really was.

Adam Roberts says of *Swastika Night*, 'Burdekin's pre-war story reads as horribly prescient and its feminist emphasis ... provides a very valid critique of fascism.' Largely forgotten, it gained a new lease of life when it was republished in the 1980s.

TEDDYBÄR

!!!

An odd trend swept through Germany in the 1920s, and continued for another forty years – individuals and crowds posing for the camera with people dressed in polar bear costumes. The bizarre pictures may have never seen the light of day but are known to us thanks to collector Jean-Marie Donat, who collected the photographs for a limited edition book, *TeddyBär*.

Various pictures survive, those posing with the polar bears including German soldiers, a holidaying family at the Baltic Sea, a young girl who is in the League of German Maidens uniform and the after-service of a wedding. Later pictures include posing with black GIs and youngsters from what appears to be the Swinging Sixties.

What is weirdest here is that the reasons for the polar bear phenomena aren't clear. Unsatisfactory answers include: links to the soft drink Fanta as a mascot; the belief that polar bears were simply popular in the country; or the idea the costumes would encourage people to have their photograph taken with a stranger. A theory it was all to celebrate the arrival of a polar bear at Berlin Zoo doesn't stand up well to scrutiny either.

Attempting to explain this oddity Jean-Marie Donat said, 'These photographs were found during 20 years of research, all over Germany, in shops that sell old photos, or in markets dating from 1920 to 1960. All these individual moments add up to the story of Germany over 40 years.'

THE TITANIC

!!

Joseph Goebbels was the head of Nazi propaganda, minister for the majestically named *Reichsministerium für Volksaufklärung und Propaganda* (Reich Ministry of Public Enlightenment and Propaganda). Goebbels' style was haphazard and often disastrous. His Degenerate Art Exhibition, mocking modern art, was ironically a raging success. He used a Jazz band to broadcast Nazi songs, to the amusement of Churchill and others, and many of his works were counter-productive – and harmful to Hitler's message.

The sinking of the RMS *Titanic*, which resulted in the death of 1,500 people on 15th April 1912, became a worldwide tragedy. The sinking of the 'ship that couldn't be sunk' sent shockwaves around the world and is perhaps, to this day, the best known seaborne disaster to many.

Ignoring the fact there already was a 1929 German filmed 'Atlantik' telling the story of the ill-fated ship, Goebbels decided he wanted it filmed again. In 1943, 'Titanic' was released. This version added an entirely fictitious German hero, First Officer Peterson, and blamed the sinking on Western capitalism. The film's director, Helbert Selpin, who was frustrated with the drunken actions of the extras on set, was arrested for his off-colour remarks and detained. Later that same day he was found hanged in his prison cell, whether this was murder or suicide isn't entirely clear though murder seems much more likely.

Oddly, this movie, having cost 4 million Reichmarks to make, was then suppressed by Goebbels, who realised that showing more tragedy, despair and panicked people desperately looking for their families could be detrimental to the spirits of the German audience. Particularly as they were suffering air raids themselves.

Ironically, the ship used for the film was the SS *Cap Arcona*, which would suffer a tragedy even greater than the real life Titanic disaster.

Cap Arcona, known as 'the floating palace', would later be used in 1945 as part of Operation Hannibal to evacuate soldiers and civilians from East Prussia to West Germany and away from the advancing Red Army. The journeys across the Baltic Sea would have been terrifying, with the ships constantly being hunted by Soviet submarines and the perennial threat of mines. The greatest maritime disaster in history, the sinking of the *Wilhelm Gustloff* and costing 10,000 lives, took place during these evacuations.

So nerve-wracking must these journeys have been that in February 1945 the ship's captain, Johannes Gertz, shot himself in his cabin rather than endure another trip across the Baltic when he was ordered to go back East.

And, of course, a ship linked to the cursed RMS *Titanic*, was never going to escape the war unscathed.

It was 3rd May 1945. Hitler was dead and the remnants of the Nazi leadership were in flight. Intelligence had reached the British that the Nazi and SS leaders were gathered at Flensburg in Germany, preparing to sail to Norway aboard the SS *Cap Arcona* and a few other ships. They hoped to escape by disappearing into society where they could live unpunished and return to a normal existence. To aid their getaway, they 'unburdened' themselves of the concentration camp prisoners that were with them. The emaciated corpses of their victims – men, women, children – soon littered the foreshore. Heinrich Himmler was there, and his intentions were clear. A signed note from 14th April 1945 read, 'no prisoner must be allowed to fall into the hands of the enemy alive.'

This was it, the day of wrath and justice. The sadistic Nazis who had orchestrated a six-year war leaving tens of millions dead, were gathered in one place at the same time. This would be like shooting fish in a barrel, it was too good to be true.

Squadrons of RAF Hawker Typhoons attacked *Cap Arcona* and the flotilla at Lubeck Bay, dropping their bombs and strafing the survivors in the water without mercy. *Cap Arcona* caught on fire and capsized.

The tragedy is, the RAF didn't know the full story. These ships actually *were* laden with concentration camp survivors. Crucial information from the Red

Cross that a mass of survivors were present on the ships had not reached the RAF pilots. The poor souls had survived years of anguish, only to be drowned or shot by their liberators. 7,400 prisoners were killed. Of the 5,000 aboard the *Cap Arcona*, only 350 were saved. It was the stuff of nightmares – the survivors ran the gauntlet of drowning or being shot at by the SS and the mistaken RAF at the same time.

This depressingly tragic event is even harder to bear when you realise that the war in Europe ended only a few days later, on 8th May 1945. For the prisoners this must have been an unbearably horrific finale to the Second World War. Theories survive that the British kept this incident secret from both the pilots and the public, and it should have been sealed for 100 years, not being released to the population until 2045, but it was de-classified early for unknown reasons. What is more likely is that the details of the incident were released in 1972 after the Public Records Act 1967 reduced the amount of time similar state records were to be kept classified. The remains of victims of this tragedy continued to wash up on land as late as 1971.

Having said all that, there is one aspect that should not be forgotten. Despite obvious denials from the Nazi survivors, who sought to mitigate their actions and plans, there was clear and corroborated testimony during the subsequent war trials that, had the Nazis actually completed their journey across the North Sea, they had a plan to ensure their security. This was simply to blow up the three vessels while all the prisoners remained on board. It's unlikely the ships were even seaworthy. It would appear that the only reason why they were loaded aboard in the first place was not in order to sustain their lives, but so the Allies could not interrogate them and hear their damning personal accounts. The three vessels would have sunk with the 10,000 prisoners sealed within, dying from the explosions, from drowning, or asphyxiation. This final crime would have been covered up - presented as an unfortunate accident or a regrettable incident of friendly fire, assuming the Allies had not got to them first.

THAT'S ALL FOLKS!

!!

Propaganda was considered a crucial part of the war effort for all sides of the conflict. Efforts to encourage public support for a cause and demonise an enemy, have existed since the first word was written. However, what was unique about the Second World War was the sheer intensity of it. Soldiers and civilians were bombarded constantly, and unlike earlier wars, which were usually fought in a field far-away, this war was unavoidable.

Propaganda even found its way into children's cartoons. The list is far too long to detail here, but hundreds of cartoons were created throughout the six-year conflict. The use of propaganda, and the manner in which it was presented, is fascinating. It reveals that the war was never a simple case of good and evil, black and white. A close friend and ally one moment could be a bitter enemy the next, and vice versa.

Der Fuehrer's Face is a 1943 cartoon featuring Donald Duck having a bad dream - he dreams that he's a Nazi. Interestingly, this cartoon was temporarily banned as extremist material by a

Russian court – in 2010! Spike Jones' song of the same name became a favourite for the soldiers.

Herr Meets Hare and *Bugs Bunny Nips the Nips* were two outings for the Warner Bros animal. The former generally sees him irritating the Nazis, particularly Goering 'the golden pheasant'; the latter sees him outsmarting the Japanese.

The more sensible and compassionate *Education for Death: The Making of the Nazi*, follows a newborn baby named Hans through his brainwashed childhood and depicts German children as victims.

Comic books heroes also joined the fight; DC and Marvel Comics stalwarts Wonder Woman, Superman, Captain America, Daredevil, Batman and Flash Gordon were constantly fighting the bad guys. Superman, the Man of Steel – the fact that he shared his name with 'Uncle Joe' Stalin is notable here – was already punching Nazis a year before America joined the war. Some cartoons of Asian people were so ridiculous they would be funny, were they not so racist.

It wasn't just the Allies who were hurling their propaganda messages at children; the Axis was doing the same. *Nimbus Libere* from 1944 is a very odd, short cartoon, made by the Germans but aimed at the French. In this Mickey Mouse, Popeye and Donald Duck are the crew of Allied bombers, promising the French salvation, but instead kill them in a bombing run.

The Italian cartoon *Il Dottor Churkill* sees Winston Churchill as a deranged Dr. Jekyll and Mr. Hyde type monster, a greedy sociopath who lives in the Bank of England and robs his friends, before being defeated by a combined Italian and German airforce.

Momotarō no Umiwashi (Momotarō's Sea Eagles) was a 1942 contribution showing the attack on the 'Devil's Island' (Pearl Harbor). Bluto, the nemesis of Popeye – now a drunk sailor - defends the US.

Perhaps the most peculiar, though, is *Omochabako series dai san wa: Ehon senkya-hyakusanja-rokunen* (Mickey Mouse invades Japan). A monstrous Mickey Mouse terrorises Japanese children before eventually being defeated by a samurai. This cartoon stands out for special attention because it was actually made by the Japanese in 1936, five years before the nations were even at war with each other.

THERESIENSTADT – THE MODEL VILLAGE

!

While the war continued in Germany's favour, news of the existence of concentration camps, ghettos and the brutal treatment of civilians under their control did not particularly concern the Nazis.

But as the tide of war turned and the Allies made inroads into Europe, the situation changed. It dawned on SS and Nazi leaders that perhaps they may be held accountable for their inhumanity and cruelty after all.

After the D-Day landings, their concerns increased. The international community wanted to know if so-called extermination camps existed – surely they couldn't? Surely, they were just ridiculous lies to demonise the Third Reich? The first Danish Jews had arrived in 1943, and facing increasing pressure from the Danish Red Cross, the Nazis finally allowed the charity to investigate the claims. They were to be permitted to visit Theresienstadt, a camp, they were told, which was representative of all the others dotted throughout Europe.

The Nazis went into overdrive in preparation for the visit. They deported a large number to Auschwitz to show the camps weren't overcrowded. Orphans and the sick were removed – they'd be a depressing sight. It was cleaned up, fake shops and cafes were built. Flowers were planted, benches and playgrounds were created. The residents who were to be visited had freshly painted homes, no more than three to a room.

The Red Cross visit was on 23rd June 1944. Following a very specific route on their tour, they were apparently impressed by conditions in the camp, young ones sang and danced, the smell of bread wafted from the bakery, and the scent of the newly planted flowers filled the air. They even attended a children's performance of *Brundibár*. What was all the fuss about? The tales of the shocking, brutal treatment of Jews was all an absurd lie. In the First World War the Allies had accused the Germans of rendering corpses to make oils for the war effort. This was, in reality, a complete fabrication. The Danes knew that the British had lied before, why should they be trusted now? The Red Cross left contentedly, and the ruse worked

After the visit, a propaganda film was made of the seemingly lovely conditions at Theresienstadt, directed by an inmate Kurt Gerron, an experienced director and actor who had previously worked with Marlene Dietrich. Naturally, after the film was made, Gerron and the cast and crew were murdered at Auschwitz. Only 17,000 were left when the camp was finally liberated, the Red Cross briefly taking over administration on 2nd May 1945. The complete film of this disturbingly fake toy-town no longer exists, but some footage has survived.

TIMUR'S CURSE

!!

Timur, or Tamerlane (Timur the Lame), was a 14th century Turco-Mongol ruler. The Great Khan of 1369 is remembered as the last of the great nomadic conquerors. An estimated 17 million people were killed under his brutal reign. On his death during a campaign to China, he was entombed in the Gur-e-Amir mausoleum in Samarkand, Uzbekistan.

But what does any of this have to do with World War Two?

A legend says that Timur's tomb bore two inscriptions. The first read, 'When I rise from the dead, the world shall tremble,' while the second, on his casket, read, 'Whosoever disturbs my tomb will unleash an invader more terrible than I.'

On 19th June 1941, Soviet anthropologists opened the tomb to examine his remains. Operation Barborossa, the largest military assault in history, was unleashed against the Soviet Union three days later.

Timur was reburied and put to rest in November 1942, soon after the Soviets were victorious and turned the tide of the war after the pivotal Battle of Stalingrad.

This legend does run in a similar manner to that of the curse of the Egyptian pharaoh Tutankhamun, which did in fact throw up some very odd coincidences. Even the most skeptical among us must admit that it's a great story at least. Gur-e-Amir has since been renovated and remains a popular tourist attraction.

TRUST NO FOX

!

'Trau keinem Fuchs auf grüner Heid und keinem Jud auf seinem Eid' or 'Trust No Fox in the Green Meadow and No Jew on His Oath', was a children's book written by 18-year-old kindergarten teacher Elvira Bauer and illustrated by Philipp Rupprecht.

It was published in 1936 by Sturmer-Verlag, run by chief Nazi propagandist Julius Streicher. It saw seven editions and 100,000 copies produced and was distributed to schools throughout Germany, aimed primarily at children around six-years-old.

The content of the book is, frankly, appalling, and the fact it was read in schools to impressionable youngsters makes it all the more grim. The title itself comes from a quotation of Martin Luther's, the leader of the Protestant reformation in 1543.

The colourful and bright book glosses over the usual Nazi diatribe we have come to recognise. A poem accompanies each page and image, riddled with the usual racist nonsense. According to this title, Jews are the children of the devil (Jews in fact don't believe in the devil in the Christian sense, believing humans are capable of making enough evil on their own), and they murdered Jesus. An explanation of Jewish naming customs is looked at to allow children to 'catch out' Jews. A baptised and assimilated Jew is still an insidious double agent. They are naturally greedy, filthy, lecherous. Worse, they are, paradoxically, lazy and parasitic –yet also wealthy and cruelly industrious. Jewish doctors delay the death of their patients for as long as they can, knowing each Jew is bound straight for hell.

Before Jews were completely segregated from 'Aryan' schools in 1938, the children suffered what surely must be every parent's worst nightmare. Innocent Jewish children would be forced to stand at the front of the class to be humiliated: discussed and jeered at by their teachers. The children would naturally find themselves the victims of bullying and beatings by other students as a result. This happened more than perhaps we'd like to admit, because by 1937, 97% of teachers were members of the National Socialist Teachers League. The 1938 segregation didn't give the Jewish children any reprieve either, the more fanatical youngsters of the Hitler Youth would wait outside these schools to beat up the children.

'Trust No Fox', together with two other equally disgusting and disturbing books, would be used as evidence at the Nuremberg trials. Julius Streicher was hanged in 1946, as for Elvira Bauer, well, we may assume she skulked back into normal life unpunished, if she survived the war.

U-1206

!

U-Boats, the predatory submarines of the Reich, were the terror of all sailors during the war. It was particularly the case for the Merchant Navy, whose mariners made their nerve-wracking journeys across the Atlantic, bringing food and supplies from the US to keep Britain fed, supplied and equipped. The U-Boats could strike unseen and without warning, their victims who survived the initial blast would, if there was no help in sight, very likely freeze to death in the icy waters. Churchill himself is quoted as saying 'The only thing that ever really frightened me during the war was the U-boat peril.'

As the war progressed, the Allies became increasingly more efficient at deterring, detecting and fighting back against this menace. Though there was one U-Boat, U-1206, which the Allies would themselves never have to face.

6th April 1945 saw U-1206 set off on patrol from occupied Norway. Its mission was to hunt and destroy Allied shipping. For U-Boat crews themselves, life was dangerous and thoroughly unpleasant. Living for days in cramped and squalid conditions, even tasks such as using the toilet needed to be carefully thought out in order to avoid causing danger. In emergencies, the crew had to use buckets, which couldn't be emptied until the submarine next surfaced. The smell of urine, faeces, human body odor and diesel must have been overwhelming.

The U-1206 had a new and improved plumbing system, but it was complex, and the flushing of the toilets could only be performed by specialists. While hunting shipping off the coast of Scotland, Captain Karl Adolf Schlitt had to go and relieve himself. Rather than call on one of his specialists, he attempted to operate the toilet. Failing, he eventually called for a specialist to flush it after him, but at this point his embarrassment appears to have turned into a disaster. The wrong valve was opened, and water poured into the submarine. At risk of flooding and sinking, the submariners were horrified when inrushing seawater overwhelmed the battery bank.

Soon noxious fumes of chlorine gas from the batteries filled the hull. As the air became unbreathable, the Captain had to order the vessel to surface. But here, it was a sitting duck. Allied forces soon discovered her and attacked. Four crewmen died before Captain Schlitt gave the order to abandon ship. He and the remaining forty-six crew were captured and taken prisoner.

It could be argued that the malfunctioning toilet (or operator) saved the lives of the majority of Schlitt's crew, because living onboard an U-boat was perilous: only 25% of U-Boat sailors survived the war.

Never, in the field of human conflict, was so much owed, by one flush, to one loo.

UNROTATED PROJECTILE

!!!

The Second World War saw conflict of a scale never seen before, for this was not a war of land or sea. For the first time the air became a hotly contested battle zone. As well as the dreaded U-boats, the Royal Navy understood perfectly the terrible threat posed by the Luftwaffe and the Japanese air force.

Normal air defences included batteries of 4" and 40mm guns. As always with technology, the next advancement was sought. The enigmatically named 'unrotated projectile' was the cover name for a new concept: twenty smoothbore tubes which would fire spin-stabilised rockets. Thus they were 'unrotated' unlike most other rockets.

This weapon deserves a mention as the rockets weren't aimed at aircraft, but some distance in front of them. The rockets would launch, and at a preset height detonate a small charge. This would release an 8.4 ounce mine which was itself attached to three parachutes on a 400ft wire. The concept was that, as a plane snagged the wires, it would become tangled, or, better, draw the explosives into contact with the aircraft's fuselage or wings.

The idea of an aerial minefield is sound, but the unrotated projectile didn't impress the Royal Navy. If the enemy dodged the wires, the minefield was useless. During a demonstration of the weapon at Scapa Flow, a change of wind meant that some of the mines flew back towards the vessel, becoming entangled in its rigging. Fortunately these were dummy rounds and there were no casualties.

The most famous ship to have the weapon was HMS *Hood*, which was sunk by the pride of the *Kriegsmarine*, the seemingly indestructible Bismarck. Anti-aircraft weapons advanced at an astonishing rate, but the unrotated projectile was scrapped.

THE VICTORY PARADE

!

The London Victory Celebrations of 1946 was a time of joy and jubilation; six long and hard years of war were finally over. The Allies had defeated Nazi Germany, Imperial Japan, Italy and all of the minor Axis powers. Britain, the United States, France, China and countless other nations joined in the merriment, but there was a darker side to the parade.

The Soviet Union had an ambiguous position within the Allied nations and the other countries were rather ambivalent in their feelings towards the Russian Bear. Originally friendly to Germany, the Soviets secretly carved up eastern Europe with the Nazis in the Molotov-Ribbentrop pact, and only joined the Allies out of necessity after the shock of the German onslaught of Operation Barbarossa in June 1941.

The elephant in the room was Poland. The attack on the nation by the Nazis sparked the Second World War in September 1939, but the Soviets themselves attacked from the east a few weeks later, eventually meeting the Germans at Brest-Litovsk. It was to become the German/Soviet border. The Polish put up a brave defence, but ultimately their position was untenable and their armed forces crumbled in the face of being attacked on both fronts. The Polish government-in-exile continued to function from London, with over 200,000 Poles fighting for the British throughout the course of the war. As the war was ending, it was clear that the nations between Germany and Russia would not see a return of democracy, but would fall, as Churchill prophesied, under an 'iron curtain' of puppet Soviet governments.

By 1946 tensions between East and West were already growing, and the first icy snowflakes of the impending Cold War could be felt. Political pragmatism forced the British to recognize the new communist government of Poland and the Soviets refused to allow the Poles to attend the victory celebrations. The Soviets themselves declined the invitation.

Britain and France had gone to war in 1939 to protect their ally, Poland, and her sovereignty. But after six years of war, the world had changed. Imperialist Europe was no longer top dog, having been replaced by the superpowers of the United States and the Soviet Union, and Poland would remain behind the iron curtain until 1989.

THE VON TRAPP FAMILY

!

All of us who have seen and heard *The Sound of Music* will be familiar with the Von Trapp family. The charming 1965 movie received criticism for its historical inaccuracies, but considering it was a Hollywood musical adaptation of a Broadway musical adaptation of a German film adaptation of Maria Von Trapp's book, that is hardly surprising!

Maria Kutschera was born in Vienna, Austria in 1905. In 1925, she became a nun at Nonnberg abbey in Salzburg. By 1926, sister Maria became a tutor to one of the children of Georg Von Trapp, a widowed former U-boat captain. She excelled at her work and eventually took on the other six children.

Georg became enamored of Maria and asked for her hand in marriage. Just one minor problem – she was a nun! Maria panicked and returned to her mother abbess for advice. The mother abbess reassured her she should follow her heart and that it was God's will. She left the sisterhood, accepted the marriage proposal, and moved in with the family in their home at Villa Trapp. Georg and Maria had three children of their own, bringing the number of their brood up to ten.

However not everything was rosy, the family were in dire straits financially. They had to dismiss their servants and rent out various rooms in their home to make ends meet. Then along came Father Franz Wasner to act as their chaplain. He heard the Von Trapps singing and encouraged them to pursue a professional singing career. They took his advice, and the 'Trapp Family Choir' was formed. They sang at concerts and festivals, and even on the radio.

The family's budding musical career began to develop against the backdrop of growing anti-Semitism following Hitler's 1938 *Anschluss*, the annexation of the country. Hitler, of course, was himself Austrian, not German, and had long wished to see Austria formally attached to 'Greater' Germany. Georg was now in a difficult position. He was inducted into the *Kriegsmarine*, but he despised the Nazis and what they stood for. Torn, he refused his commission, but he knew that both he and his family would be at risk of arrest and persecution. So in 1938 he and the rest of the family fled − first to Italy, then England, and finally settling in America at Vermont, New England. Their successful musical career continued for decades.

As for their old home, Trapp Villa ended up in Heinrich Himmler's hands. The picturesque building was covered in barbed wire, draped in swastikas and filled with SS guards. It was to become Himmler's summer vacation home.

In modern times, Trapp Villa has since been

restored to its former glory and is now one of the most popular tourist attractions in Austria. The Von Trapp family's story and *The Sound of Music*, continue to charm the world.

WAR AGAINST THE POTATO BEETLE

!

Autumn 1940: things were going well for the Axis. France had fallen, and only Britain – hiding beyond the English Channel – stood in opposition to them. However, they were confident the Luftwaffe's attacks would soon bring the British to submission. In the meantime, there was another enemy on the horizon which would either have to fall in line or be crushed, the potato beetle.

The Colorado bug first appears to have had a run in with potato plants around 1859, sweeping east and destroying American crops. The Americans warned Europe about the bug, and imports were stopped, but it was too little, too late and by 1877 the bug was firmly established in Europe. The devastation was so great that in the First World War the French looked into weaponising the insect against the Germans. In the Second World War, the Germans tried doing the same to the French. Allegedly, the Nazis researched the bug in controlled facilities, and tested it on themselves near Frankfurt in 1943. It has been claimed that the British ordered 12,000 from the Americans. Whatever the truth of that, the bug ate both nation's crops – neither nation deployed it as a weapon, and it wasn't taking sides.

After the war, East Germany, now under communist rule, became infested – possibly as a result of the Frankfurt test. The pro-Stalin nation called the bug 'Amikfaer', the American beetle, as the cold war was crystalizing. The Soviet agents of propaganda got their hands on this one, American capitalist planes were secretly dropping the bug on farms to starve out the inhabitants. The beetle was even compared to the atomic bomb, America's nightmarish weapon of mass destruction. Though the bugs were smaller, it was a weapon of 'US imperialists' – no doubt the work of the CIA. Farmers had to spend countless hours picking the eggs and bugs by hand, community bug killing days were launched – and the Young Pioneers youth movement did their bit too.

The Colorado bug still occupies America and Europe and has been the bane of gardeners ever since. Though have they now switched allegiance from the CIA to the KGB? In the troubles in Ukraine from 2014 onwards, the term *kolorady*, referring to the beetle, is used disparagingly to refer to pro-Russian separatists.

WHITE ROSE

!

The White Rose was a German resistance group made up of academics who opposed Nazi rule by non-violent means, using graffiti and the written word to spread their message.

Their first known actions were in 1942 in Munich, when they distributed around 15,000 pamphlets warning people of the atrocities and crimes being committed by the government.

They produced seven leaflets in total, with poignant messages such as:

'Why do you allow these men who are in power to rob you, step by step, openly and in secret, of one domain of your rights after another, until one day nothing, nothing at all will be left but a mechanised state system presided over by criminals and drunks? Is your spirit already so crushed by abuse that you forget it is your right − or rather, your moral duty − to eliminate this system?'

Though brave and commendable, it was only a

matter of time before the police and the Gestapo caught up with them. Those found to be members of the White Rose could expect brutal treatment: punishment and the farcical show trials of the 'People's Court'. Of those caught, many were executed, some of their number beheaded by guillotine, including the heroic siblings Hans and Sophie Scholl.

Despite the end they suffered, their message was not forgotten. The final leaflet produced by the small but dedicated team of the White Rose made it into the hands of the Allies. In July 1943 they dropped millions of copies from planes, scattering them and their message over Germany and the dwindling Reich.

Sophie Scholl is a hero in Germany to this day. Lillian Garrett-Groag, a playwright, summarized her thoughts of the White Rose on 22nd February 1993:

'It is possibly the most spectacular moment of resistance that I can think of in the twentieth century. The fact that five little kids, in the mouth of the wolf, where it really counted, had the tremendous courage to do what they did, is spectacular to me. I know that the world is better for them having been there, but I don't know why.'

WHO, ME?

!!!

A top-secret, war-winning weapon was being developed by the British SOE (Special Operations Executive.) Correspondence from August 4, 1943 between British Intelligence Officer TR Bird and his American counterpart Stanley Lovell from the OSS (Office of Strategic Services) discusses the development of 'S Liquid', the S standing for stench!

The plan was for the S Liquid to be given to resistance agents in occupied Europe, who would then secretly pour it onto the clothing of Axis forces. The humiliated victims would then smell so bad they would be scorned and mocked by their comrades.

TR Bird said of the weapon, 'Since the air in any ordinary public meeting room is generally free from smell, almost any strange smell which cannot readily be accounted for would arouse suspicion which might easily culminate in fear or even panic.'

The Americans were impressed, and planned their own variant known as Who, Me? or Why Me? spending two years working on a weapon with 'the revolting odour of a very loose bowel movement'.

The weapon didn't quite go to plan; the S Liquid was highly volatile and unpredictable. The attacker would often end up smelling as bad as, or worse than, their victim. It was abandoned two weeks later.

WILLIAM LONKOWSKI

!!

U nravelling the facts and fiction from the murky world of espionage is often a near-impossible and ultimately futile task. Truths, half-truths, confusion, deliberate lies, rumours and omissions are hopelessly intertwined. Despite this, many espionage stories are known to us.

One such case was that of William Lonkowski, a German *Abwehr* agent, operating in the United States. Lonkowski found work in Long Island, New York at the Ireland Aircraft Corporation. He began feeding back vital plans and information to his handlers, and soon befriended two German-Americans, Otto Voss and Werner Gudenberg, who joined his spy ring. His next cover was taking on a job with *Luftreise*, a German aviation magazine.

Lonkowski almost slipped up on 25th September 1935. He was stopped by a customs official as he was boarding the ocean liner *Europa*. Within Lonkowski's violin case, a favourite of fictional spies ever since, were aircraft drawings. He was interviewed by military authorities and explained he needed the pictures for his magazine article. He was told to return three days later. He didn't bother. Instead he went to Canada and headed home on a German freighter. He received a hero's welcome.

Is any of this true? What really happened? Welcome to the shadowy world of espionage. *Confessions of a Nazi Spy*, (1939) Hollywood's first anti-Nazi film was inspired, in part along with the Rumrich spy case, by Lonkowski.

WINDKANONE

!

As the war progressed, Hitler became increasingly obsessed with his *wunderwaffe*; his wonder weapons, which he believed, would miraculously turn the course of the war back in his favour. Many prototypes and ideas were floated: most were either unworkable, dismal failures or simply an unacceptable diversion of men and resources that could be better placed elsewhere.

One of the most odd weapons of the wunderwaffe arsenal, but one which was actually made, was the *Windkanone* (Wind Cannon). It was an anti-aircraft weapon developed in Stuttgart that fired a jet of compressed air and water vapour, similar to the effects of turbulence, designed to assault enemy planes. The idea behind this was that the weapon could knock down low-flying aircraft, without needing ammunition. A wind cannon was installed on a bridge over the River Elbe in 1945, but we have no evidence of its effectiveness.

The weapon was scientifically impressive in a sense, but the war ended before the windkanone was capable of doing much more than smashing 25mm thick wooden planks from a distance of 200m – itself hardly enough to turn the tide.

WINKIE THE PIGEON

!!

2 3rd February 1942 saw a Bristol Beaufort bomber, having sustained severe damage, crash into the merciless North Sea. The crew were stranded 100 miles from home, their odds of survival were next to nothing – with no points of reference, and struggling in the freezing waters, the men could not radio their position.

But the four men still had one hope – a pigeon named Winkie. The blue chequered hen bird was set loose, in the faint hope it could make it back to its home in Broughty Ferry, Scotland.

Against all the odds, Winkie did make it home, after flying 120 miles, exhausted and covered in oil – but Winkie wasn't carrying a message. Remarkably, the RAF calculated the time difference between the bomber crashing and the pigeon arriving, allowing for wind direction and the bird being covered in oil, and were able to pinpoint where the Bristol Beaufort crashed.

A rescue mission was launched and the crew, resigned to their fates, were saved within fifteen minutes, in what must have been a time of elation. Back at base, a dinner was held in her honour. She received the Dickin Medal on 2nd December 1943 for 'delivering a message under exceptional difficulties'.

WINTON'S CHILDREN

!

He was an unlikely hero, a stock broker from London: Nicholas Wertheimer. He had been born in 1909 to German Jew parents, but in an effort to integrate with their new society, they anglicized their surname to Winton and converted to Christianity.

When Hitler's grip began to tighten over Germany, life became increasingly unbearable for Jews. It was never going to be as simple as 'just leaving'; they had families, friends, homes, careers. Emigrating was expensive, so most couldn't afford it. Besides, other countries had strict immigration quotas – British Mandate Palestine was political dynamite, so they couldn't go there either. As one survivor would later state, the world was divided into countries where they couldn't stay and countries they couldn't go.

It was December 1938 and time for the stockbroker to take a well-deserved holiday, the skiing in Switzerland was excellent and would make a perfect getaway. But before he left, he received a chance letter in the post., It was from an old friend

Martin Blake, who was in Prague. 'I have a most interesting assignment and I need your help. Don't bother bringing your skis.' He accepted Blake's invitation and headed to Prague.

Prague shocked Winton, the appalling conditions not just of the Jews, but of all the refugees who were fleeing in the face of Nazi Germany's annexation of the Sudetenland. Winton set up an organisation, linked to the *kindertransport* program, to help Jewish children at risk of the growing anti-Semitism. Thanks to the pressure of humanitarian groups and the Quakers, Britain agreed to take them in temporarily until the crisis was over, provided a home could be found for them.

We can only imagine the real desperation and despair of the parents, to allow their children to go off unaccompanied to the other side of Europe, through the heartland of the Reich, and into the arms of strangers. Innocently naïve children would occasionally give them Hitler salute as they left.

There were still hurdles, the Netherlands had closed its borders to Jewish refugees and the police would send back any refugees they discovered. Eventually the Netherlands got on board and allowed the safe passage of the children through their country to reach Britain.

The effort was overwhelming, but Winton and his friends worked tirelessly to advertise the plight of the children and find caring homes for them. His own mother helped out. Time was ticking, Winton sent a plea for help out to the world, and to Roosevelt's United States in particular, but it fell on deaf ears. Only Sweden agreed to join Britain and assist.

Winton's work in Prague came to an end on 1st September with the outbreak of the war. Tragically, the last trainload of 250 children which was due to set off was unable to depart due to wartime restrictions. Of these 250 children, only two survived the war. However some 10,000 children escaped the clutches of the Nazis through the *kindertransport* program, and Winton himself personally saved 669 of them.

With the war beginning in 1939, Winton first joined up as a conscientious objector with the Red Cross. He had a change of heart in 1940, when he discovered he had the strength within him to fight.

Winton's story is remarkable enough. He was one of the untold humble heroes of the war. But there was a surprise in store for him.

It was 1988, four decades since the war had ended, and Winton's wife Grete was having a rummage in their attic. While doing so, she came across a peculiar scrapbook, inside which were the names and addresses of all the kind souls who had agreed to take Winton's children in. It also contained the names and addresses of the children's parents. Winton didn't remember this scrapbook. 'Isn't that odd,' they must have thought, to have forgotten that they had it.

He was knighted in 2003. 2008 saw him receive the Pride of Britain award. Two years later he was named as a British Hero of the Holocaust. A statue of the altruistic hero with a couple of his children still stands at Prague railway station, mingled in with the hustle and bustle of the modern world.

It is believed that 370 of Winton's children have never been traced, and probably remain oblivious of their own past.

Winton died peacefully in his sleep at the age of 106 in 2015, 76 years to the day that 241 of his children, because of his kindness and hard work, left certain death behind them at the platform.

WOJTEK THE BEAR

!!

Operation Barbarossa, the surprise Axis invasion of the Soviet Union changed everything. For the Allies, the Soviet Union turned from an enemy to a friend.

The Soviet Union had joined the Nazis in carving up Eastern Europe in 1939, and many Polish soldiers and deported civilians found themselves in brutal gulags as a result. With the Reich closing in on the Soviet Union in 1941, they released the Polish prisoners, who set off for Iran, nominally independent but in reality ruled by the British.

On their journey, the Poles came across a young Iranian boy near the town of Hamadan, the boy had a bear cub with him, after hunters had shot its mother. Lt. Anatol Tarnowiecki was taken in by the bear. The bear spent three months with the group at the Polish refugee camp near Tehran.

In August 1942 the bear was donated to the 22nd Artillery Company and given the name Wojtek (Happy Warrior). Wojtek fitted in well with his comrades, he was rather fond of food and enjoyed marmalade, honey and syrup and even shared cigarettes, though he sometimes preferred to eat them rather than smoke them. He liked play fighting and was taught to salute and joined the soldiers' journey, without complaint, through Syria, Palestine and Egypt.

When the Polish were to join the British in the Italian campaign, Wojtek was officially enlisted with the rank of private, to ensure his place on a transport ship. He received a pay book and rations, although any pay was substituted with double rations.

During the battle of Monte Cassino, Wojtek did his part by carrying 100 pound crates of shells to the gun crews. In fact the image of Wojtek carrying a shell became the official symbol of 22 Company.

After the war Wojtek retired to Britain. He lived at Edinburgh Zoo, where old Polish comrades would continue to sneak him cigarettes, but he didn't have matches or a lighter so he would have to eat them.

He was featured on the children's program *Blue Peter*. Wojtek's popularity never diminished, and countless statues and tributes have been paid to him, the most recent being a 2015 statue in Princes Street Gardens in Edinburgh.

WOLFSKINDER

!

War is not neat, it doesn't 'end' on an arbitrary date. The tremors continue. Post-war Europe and Asia were chaotic, and soldiers didn't go home for years as they were sent to occupy conquered countries and uphold the law. Millions of homeless refugees streamed to and fro, while civilians wandered desperately, trying to discover news of family and friends. Some scars, physical and emotional, would last for decades; some would never heal at all, and followed the victims to their graves.

Among the dead were countless German parents. Many orphans, who may once have been in children's homes or other institutions, now found themselves without any care at all. Thousands of these children were slaughtered by bombs and reprisals, so for some the best bet was to take their chances in the wild by foraging, begging and stealing. Others had sick or dying parents, and it was up to the children to care for them.

These groups of wandering semi-feral children

became known as *wolfskinder* (wolf children). As the children were German, the Soviets would punish harshly any adults found to be caring for them. Children who were caught were often deported East, many of whom would not survive the journey. Despite this, many adults took a risk and did help, particularly in rural farms. Lithuania alone took in around 45,000 wolf children.

It was only in 1991, after the fall of the Soviet Union, that the wolfskinder and their carers were free to reveal the children's identities without reprisals. However, 45 years had passed, and the children were now adults themselves. In later years, some would look in vain for any information about their old lives and family, while many more were oblivious to their past.

YANG KYOUNGJONG

!

Yang Kyoungjong was, allegedly, a Korean who had the dubious honor of being forced to fight for the Imperial Japanese Army, the Red Army and the Wehrmacht.

The story goes that Yang Kyoungjong was conscripted by the Japanese into the Kwangtung Army, at this time Korea was under the rule of Japan. He was sent to fight the Red Army during the border skirmishes of Khalkin Gol. Captured, he was sent to a gulag before being forcibly enlisted into the Soviet army in 1942. He was next sent to fight the Germans on the Eastern front. Again, after the battle of Kharkov, he was captured and joined the 'Eastern Battalions'. His final posting was as a guard in northern France along the Atlantic Wall. After the D-Day landings of June 1944, Yang Kyoungjong was captured one last time by the Allies.

It is claimed that after the war, he became a US citizen, living the rest of his life in Illinois before dying in 1992.

The story of Yang Kyoungjong throws up some

odd questions. If the man was real, and if he did experience what is claimed, surely someone – given how remarkable his story is, would have interviewed him, or dug up more information during his lifetime. Why is there no more information about the man's life from 1945 – 1992? A picture of an Asian soldier in German uniform has been identified as Yang Kyoungjong, but the connection is suspect. A 2005 Korean documentary questions whether the man even existed.

So is any of this true or not? Either way, the 2011 South Korean film *My Way* is based on his story.

Other titles by BLKDOG Publishing that you may enjoy:

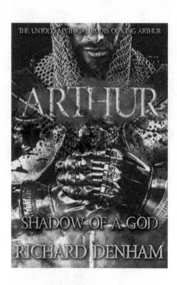

Arthur: Shadow of a God
By Richard Denham

King Arthur has fascinated the Western world for over a thousand years and yet we still know nothing more about him now than we did then. Layer upon layer of heroics and exploits has been piled upon him to the point where history, legend and myth have become hopelessly entangled.

In recent years, there has been a sort of scholarly consensus that 'the once and future king' was clearly some sort of Romano-British warlord, heroically stemming the tide of wave after wave of Saxon invaders after the end of Roman rule. But surprisingly, and no matter how much we enjoy this narrative, there is actually next-to-nothing solid to support this theory except the wishful thinking of understandably bitter contemporaries. The sources and scholarship used to support the 'real Arthur' are as much tentative guesswork and pushing 'evidence' to the extreme to fit in with this version as anything involving magic swords, wizards and dragons. Even Archaeology remains silent. Arthur is, and always has been, the square peg that refuses to fit neatly into the historians round hole.

Arthur: Shadow of a God gives a fascinating overview of Britain's lost hero and casts a light over an often-overlooked and somewhat inconvenient truth; Arthur was almost certainly not a man at all, but a god. He is linked inextricably to the world of Celtic folklore and Druidic traditions. Whereas tyrants like Nero and Caligula were men who fancied themselves gods; is it not possible that Arthur was a god we have turned into a man? Perhaps then there is a truth here. Arthur, 'The King under the Mountain'; sleeping until his return will never return, after all, because he doesn't need to. Arthur the god never left in the first place and remains as popular today as he ever was. His legend echoes in stories, films and games that are every bit as imaginative and fanciful as that which the minds of talented bards such as Taliesin and Aneirin came up with when the mists of the 'dark ages' still swirled over Britain – and perhaps that is a good thing after all, most at home in the imaginations of children and adults alike – being the Arthur his believers want him to be.

A Storm of Magic
By Ashley Laino

Being brought back from the dead is an impressive trick, even for magician Darien Burron. Now he must try and use his sleight of hand to swindle modern-day witch, Mirah, to sign her power away, or end up a tormented demon in the afterlife.

Meanwhile, sixteen-year-old Mirah is starting to lose control of her powers. After an incident at her aunt's Witchery store, Mirah is sent to a secret coven to learn to control her abilities. While away, Mirah meets up with a soft-spoken clairvoyant, a brazen storm witch, and the creator of dark magic itself. The young woman must learn to trust in herself before she loses herself entirely to the darkness that hunts her.

Click Bait
By Gillian Philip

A funny joke's a funny joke. Eddie Doolan doesn't think twice about adapting it to fit a tragic local news story and posting it on social media.

It's less of a joke when his drunken post goes viral. It stops being funny altogether when Eddie ends up jobless, friendless and ostracized by the whole town of Langburn. This isn't how he wanted to achieve fame.

Under siege from the press, and facing charges not just for the joke but for a history of abusive behavior on the internet, Eddie grows increasingly paranoid and desperate. The only people still speaking to him are Crow, a neglected kid who relies on Eddie for food and company, and Sid, the local gamekeeper's granddaughter. It's Sid who offers Eddie a refuge and an understanding ear.

But she also offers him an illegal shotgun - and as Eddie's life spirals downwards, and his efforts at redemption are thwarted at every turn, the gun starts to look like the answer to all his problems.

Burning Bridges
By Chris Bedell

They've always said that three's a crowd...

24-year-old Sasha didn't anticipate her identical twin Riley killing herself upon their reconciliation after years of estrangement. But Sasha senses an opportunity and assumes Riley's identity so she can escape her old life.

Playing Riley isn't without complications, though. Riley's had a strained relationship with her wife and stepson so Sasha must do whatever she can to make her newfound family love and accept her. If Sasha's arrangement ends, then she'll have nothing protecting her from her past. However, when one of Sasha's former clients tracks her down, Sasha must choose between her new life and the only person who cared about her.

But things are about to become even more complicated, as a third sister, Katrina, enters the scene...

Father of Storms
By Dean Jones

Imagine losing everything you loved as well as the future you'd wished for so long to come true.

Seth was born with the gift to manipulate energy, unfortunately his skills mark him as a target for one who wishes to control everything. So began a life running from those who would seek to command him, a life that spans over a thousand years waiting for the day when all will be once again as it was.

Captured in modern day London, Seth needs the help of his companions, the Mara, to show him who he is through dreams of his past, so he can save the family he has waited so long to have. A warrior bred for battle must fight once more but this time the battlefield is his mind. Can Seth win, or will he finally lose who he is and become the weapon of the man who started his nightmare all those years ago? *Father of Storms* is a story told through time, a tale of love and hope where there seems to be none and above all it is a reminder that if you believe, truly believe then even from the darkest places, good things come to those who wait.

www.blkdogpublishing.com